SALMON WEATHER

Writing from the Land of No Return

CMARIE FUHRMAN

Columbus State University
PRESS

Printed digitally

EU Authorized Representative
Easy Access System Europe—Mustamäe tee 50, 10621 Tallinn, Estonia,
gpsr.requests@easproject.com

Library of Congress Control Number: 2024947499

Published by Columbus State University Press

Marketing and distribution by UGA Press

Cover designed by Peter Selgin

Author photo by Mel Ota

Praise for *Salmon Weather*

Salmon Weather is a map to becoming, of finding oneself inside the arms of landscape, of loving and leaving and living and dying. It explores not only the deep wild of the Idaho backcountry, but the deeper wildness of the human heart. In essays both tender and unflinching, CMarie Fuhrman bears witness to stories and places, animals and people, and the profound paradoxes that have shaped her identity as an adopted Native person. In the end, this book is a love letter not only to place and a life deeply lived inside weather and seasons, but to life itself, in all its uncertainty, for all of us—to the person we were and the one we hope to become.

—**Karen Auvinen**, author of *Rough Beauty: Four Seasons of Mountain Living*

When I wonder about the weight of inheritance – about what landscapes hold, the heft of history, the texture of identity, about what my role is to steward the present for the future—I turn to CMarie Fuhrman's deft, muscular, and challenging writing. These essays are bedrock for who we've been and who we can become.

—**Taylor Brorby**, author of *Boys and Oil: Growing Up Gay in a Fractured Land*

Salmon Weather touches on matters about which I know a bit, snakes and deer hunting for example, and gets them right. These deeply moving essays amount to a shared journey, during which Fuhrman does something rare and precious—takes readers, regardless of our own immensely varied stories, onto perilous ground. Thanks to this Indigenous woman's gifted prose, an old white guy like me can better grapple with identity, fear, and loss, with love for particular places, dogs, and people, with prospects for a hopeful future.

—**Harry W. Greene**, Cornell University emeritus professor of ecology and evolution, and author of *Tracks and Shadows: Field Biology as Art*

To read a new book by CMarie Fuhrman is to experience life-changing revelations: to see mountains and waters as full of vibrant, sentient creatures; to find intimacy in the interweavings of the braids of a river and the lines of a hand; to feel a fawn's last heartbeat pulsing in a human palm; to hear how a land speaks through songs of coyotes and bugles of elk; to learn how poems and bodies can be maps to "restoration" and "restoryation" of wounded minds and scarred wilds; and to intuit, at last, the contours of a new "geography of hope."

—**Katie Ives**, author of *Imaginary Peaks: The Riesenstein Hoax and Other Mountain Dreams*

For each of the ruins that CMarie Fuhrman stunningly excavates in this gorgeous collection, she offers a formidable measure of intellect, heart, and grace. Here is a writer who refuses easy consolation and smug pontification toward the people and forces that rupture life, land, family, and culture. Here is a writer who can imagine herself the sort of survivor who both kills and cleans up, who is as open to taking responsibility as she is to pursuing transcendence. I've read Fuhrman's essays online and in the paper for years. I am thrilled to finally be able to press her long-awaited collection into the hands of all the readers who will be transformed by it.

—**Kate Lebo**, Washington State Book Award Winner, author of *Pie School, The Book of Difficult Fruit*, and *Seven Prayers*

Intense and reflective, heart-wrenching and heart-expanding, this essay collection holds contradictory and complex emotions together with tenderness and care. *Salmon Weather* offers hard-won truths and yet wonder. It is fierce and yet humane. It is honest and yet full of compassion. An ode to all things wild, these essays are written with precision and masterful prose. Readers are welcomed into this wild world—and will leave a changed person.

—**Laura Pritchett**, winner of the PEN USA Award for Fiction and author of *Three Keys*

Gorgeous, gut-wrenching, and transcendent. CMarie Fuhrman offers the reader both her arrant honesty and her giant heart. *Salmon Weather* casts a love spell.

—**Betsy Gaines Quammen**, author of *American Zion: Cliven Bundy, God, and Public Lands in the West* and *True West: Myth and Mending on the Far Side of America*

For Kim Barnes

"There are ways in, journeys to the center of life, through time; through air, matter, dream and thought. The ways are not always mapped or charted, but sometimes being lost, if there is such a thing, is the sweetest place to be. And always, in this search, a person might find that she is already there, at the center of the world. It may be a broken world, but it is glorious nonetheless."

—Linda Hogan, *The Woman Who Watches
Over the World: A Native Memoir*

*"It's dark because you are trying too hard.
Lightly child, lightly. Learn to do everything lightly.
Yes, feel lightly even though you're feeling deeply.
Just lightly let things happen and lightly cope with them."*

—Aldous Huxley, *Island*

"Every place, like every person, is elevated by the love and respect shown toward it, and by the way in which its bounty is received."

—Richard Nelson, *The Island Within*

Contents

How I Got Here and Why I've Stayed

Her cool body, a ribbon of delicate yet substantial muscle, stretched across the road. Knowing little of a snake's discomforts, I pinched her middle gently and lifted her. I placed her in my palm where she curled up as tight and small as a ball of thick yarn. In the fading light of a late May evening, my partner and I stared at the Rubber Boa, glad for another chance to spend close time with this often unseen being.

As Caleb carried her to safety, away from the mean macadam of uncaring tires, my thoughts drifted back to the first Rubber Boa I'd encountered. It was thirteen years ago, not far from this very spot, on the same Forest Service road, but 30 miles closer to town.

A laugh escapes, remembering how different I was back then. I couldn't imagine touching that first snake, let alone picking her up. I'm certain Caleb pointed out that she was a constrictor, that she wouldn't bite. He held out his open palm, assuring me there was nothing to fear. But back then, fear filled me. Not just of snakes, but of the many unknowns in this Idaho landscape that was still so new to me. Nevertheless, I was smitten. Love and fear, both equally alive within me, were kin.

Love brought me to Idaho. Love in the form of Caleb. A crisp ad on an online dating app. I read his words and thought we might be companionable but then read that he wanted to meet local girls. I was not local. I was 1,500 miles away in Northern Colorado, grieving the loss of my father. He had died just two months before, in March of 2011. Caleb wrote back, hinting he might even move for the right girl. But in the end, he wouldn't have to. On July 1, 2011, we met in Southeast Idaho. Following rivers and his white pickup truck, I eventually found my way to McCall. I came and went for a couple of months until, on the verge of fall, he said, "You should just stay here."

My life's most pivotal moments have often sprung from impulse. A fleeting thought, a spark of inspiration, a snap decision, and my entire trajectory is altered. That's been my Idaho experience, the second chapter of my life. Losing my father was a profound loss, as the death of a parent always is, but I was already in a weird transitional decade of my life. My father began showing signs of Alzheimer's while he and my mom were visiting me in June of 2004 in Montana. Had I not been so distraught with the sudden death of my husband, I may have been a better daughter to him through a time that must have been terrifying, for he was aware of his forgetting, grabbing on to stories and memories like the limbs of a tree he was falling through.

My husband, Randy, drowned in a kayaking accident on June 26, 2004. I was only 32, twenty years younger than I am now. Sometimes, I can take myself right back to that afternoon on the Clarks Fork River, north of Cody, Wyoming. I'm lying beside his lifeless body in the coroner's van. I can smell the river on his wetsuit. A hollowness creeps into me, a void that will soon consume me entirely. In a year, all that would remain was a shell, like the empty casing a caddisfly leaves when she emerges. An encasement of tiny stones meant to protect what was living inside. Yet, for me, it was the shell, not the being that emerged, that would be my body for a decade.

Then, I came to Idaho. I've always loved the coincidence of Idaho's abbreviation: ID. Identity. That, along with the vast, complex, wild, and complicated landscape—still so much a mystery to me—would help me understand who I am now. Idaho would help me forge my identity as I step into this second half of my life.

When I was growing, my father and I spent countless hours casting for Rainbow and Brook Trout, but in Idaho, I found myself lying on riverbanks, watching Steelhead and Spring Chinook carve redds into the gravel with their powerful tails. I learned to recognize the flashes of red that signaled Kokanee. More than simply identifying these and other aquatic beings continued, I came to understand their profound importance to the landscape and its people. In time, I even put aside my fishing rod, more interested in preserving the habitat that sustained these fish than in catching them for dinner.

And though I had grown up slightly feral, with a bedroom my parents built on the patio so I would stop sleeping in the grass beneath the clothesline, I have never been so deeply wild as in Idaho. Here, I've backpacked for days through the Frank Church Wilderness's remote reaches, hunted in rugged Hells Canyon, and canoed the rivers that feed and drain Payette Lake. Every year, I spend a week above Hells Canyon's last dam, following trails made by miners and packers. I venture into wolf country, startling cow elk and their calves as we traverse the hills before poison ivy and rattlesnakes awaken. My adventures have taken me across Idaho, each excursion filling me with awe. But none have been as significant as my time in the Salmon River drainages, particularly the upper South Fork. If one gets called to a natural home, I have been called to mine.

Walking the land, I have gotten to know who I am through what I stand for. Glimpsing wolves and hearing their song solidified my commitment to protecting these incredible beings. Witnessing a mother black bear defending her cubs against a larger male, urging them up a tree until the threat passed, made me a lifelong advocate for their kind. And later, when those cubs clambered down to nurse, their vulnerable bellies exposed, I understood what it means to be a writer: to bear witness, to share stories, to reveal the raw and tender truths of myself, of the world.

Another impulsive decision led me to the University of Idaho. I'd always written but with no clear path. When I saw the faculty list, even with the university three and a half hours away, I knew I had to go. I spent nearly five years there learning to transform the experiences that enlivened and haunted me into prose and poetry. Brian Blanchfield, Mary Clearman Blew, Michael McGriff, Kim Barnes, Scott Slovik, Alexandra Teague, and Robert Wrigley—each of them left an indelible mark on my journey as a writer. Perhaps it's no surprise that Kim and Bob ultimately had the most profound impact. They not only taught me the craft of writing but also instilled a deeper understanding of my own voice and how to uncover it within my work. Both are kin to Idaho, having fished the same rivers and walked the same canyons. They weave Idaho into their writing as if it were a living, breathing character. With their help, all the disparate threads of my self came together in writing that felt true. Even after I graduated in 2019, the learning continues.

Thinking back to the Rubber Boa encounter, I'm reminded of the friendship I formed with Harry W. Greene, a renowned herpetologist. Our connection came, as so many do these days, through the digital world, narrowing the gap between us despite the miles. Harry has patiently and gently educated me about snakes, understanding my well-founded terror.

My fear, of all kinds, stems from two sources: lack of knowledge and lack of experience. Harry, in his kind way, has helped address the former. As for the latter, his hand remains extended, offering guidance and reassurance. I eagerly anticipate the day we explore his desert landscapes together, encountering those beautiful, be-rattled beings without fear.

My childhood experiences created my fear of snakes. Glass canning jars where my father held them when found under rocks in our garden. My dog, Taffy, whipping Bull and Garter snakes to death, and somewhere buried in my DNA a fear of Rattlers that causes me nightmares even though I have never been bit or struck at in dreams or otherwise. I have a fear enough of Rattlers still that when asked to events in known Rattler country (which is growing by the warming year) I will ask about their populations, likelihood of encountering, and then I will lie awake sleepless in my tent waiting for the lump another woman told me she felt beneath her one night only to find the next morning (hours later!) that it was a cool, coiled Rattler, and thankful in the morning when the hard ground was all I felt.

After my recent Rubber Boa encounter, Harry sent me a paper and a kind note on the evolution of this remarkable reptile. He suggested I examine their vestigial hind legs, a reminder of their ancient lineage.

Each of our bodies tells a story. There are muscles in our hands that tell a story of being quadrupeds, though most of us are losing them. For many, there is the echo of a parent, of a lineage or ethnicity written in a facial expression, hair or eye color, or even a birthmark. I grew without any of these stories. I am adopted and the story I was given is not written on my DNA from either of the people I call Mom or Dad. My story appeared on paper. My identity, at least ethnically and in so many ways that I am only just discovering, was a document made in 1972 and handed along with me to Dolores and Ronald Fuhrman eleven months after I was born, after eleven months in orphanage and foster care.

I'm only now beginning to grasp the meaning of those words on my birth certificate and the implications of sharing them publicly. I could never dismiss it as irrelevant, for questions about my origins have always lingered. My curiosity is insatiable, leading me down philosophical rabbit holes as I ponder the narratives that shape my identity. I was raised by honest parents who never concealed my adoption or my mixed heritage. I grew up knowing I was at least part 'American Indian,' as my birth certificate stated. This fact was reinforced in childhood when I was called 'Cindian' in elementary school, and later by men who used derogatory terms or wanted to play 'cowboy and Indian.' The other parts of me were mostly Italian, the document said, from my father's side. When I was older, I would joke that I was a "Spaghetti Western."

But the joke turned serious as identity became central to my writing. In exploring the Western landscape through my work, it's impossible to ignore the pervasive Native influence on the land. As I approached my 50s, this realization grew more profound. I became acutely aware of the #MMIWG (Missing and Murdered Indigenous Women and Girls) crisis, an epidemic in the very places I frequented. I thought of the women in my bloodline—believing then that my mother was Native—and how many voices had been silenced. At the University of Idaho, I studied Nimiipuutimt, the language of the Nimiipuu (Nez Perce) people whose land I inhabited. I was fortunate to secure a job at the university working with Native students in a federally funded program designed for Native teachers who sought to keep their culture in the curriculum. Through these experiences, I gained a deeper understanding of the multifaceted nature of Native identity and the diverse experiences it encompasses. With this newfound knowledge, I felt more comfortable weaving my own Native identity into my writing, though often through the complex lens of adoption.

"You need to position yourself," the director of the university program advised one day. Her words were gentle, yet firm. She understood the need for radical honesty within the Native communities, who fought tirelessly for their rights and lands while witnessing white colleagues adopt or appropriate their culture and identity for personal gain. This sparked a series of internal panics. Initially, I wanted to erase any mention of my Native heritage from my writing. Eventually, I petitioned the courts for my adoption records and enlisted the help of a genealogist, an angel who would uncover the final piece of my identity puzzle—a piece crucial to understanding my true self and voice. This revelation transformed my original documents into a palimpsest, holding two truths at once.

In 2023, after years of celebrating the truth in my writing, finding a literary family, and working toward decolonization—finally filling the human shell I'd brought to Idaho—I was blindsided. A group had compiled an online list of individuals they deemed "pretend Indians," which included my name and photo. The details of that agonizing month will be revealed in my forthcoming memoir, *Cowbird*. But the pain lingers, even as I understand the motivations behind the list's creators. In a letter to my mentor, Kim Barnes, I declared I was leaving literature, that a job at the animal shelter awaited, and that I longed to disappear. The feeling of shattering was reminiscent of the aftermath of Randy's death. Perhaps the pain of discovering—or constructing— one's identity lies in the vulnerability of losing it. I wrote to my university supervisor and our provost, sharing the article and offering to step down if they felt it undermined our work.

I posted everything on social media—the claims, my adoption records, every piece I'd written about my adoption. I did everything short of ripping open my heart to reveal where my blood truly lived. But the well-meaning messages, laden with a pity I may have projected onto them, became overwhelming. Friends offered to intervene in ways that would only exacerbate the pain. So, I retreated. I deleted everything from my social media, withdrew into myself, drove to the Oregon coast, and waited.

Maybe these accusations were my metaphorical rattlesnakes. Just as I'd avoid rattlesnake country, choosing ignorance over understanding, I wanted to retreat from my writing life. I even considered abandoning the very landscape and community I'd grown to love, a stark departure from the life I'd built. But then, a note from Kim arrived, quoting Aldous Huxley's advice to "go lightly," but keep going.

This wasn't a spur-of-the-moment, life-altering event, but it was serendipitous. A genealogy angel named Julie, a friend whose own identity I hadn't fully understood, reached out with an offer to help me prove who I was. I spit into a tube and mailed it off. I unearthed the paperwork that had arrived from the courts two years earlier after a similar accusation and told Caleb, "It's time for me to face the dark." I opened the envelope, my heart pounding, and read. Julie's emails filled my inbox with family trees and connections. I found cousins, both close and distant. I learned the names of aunts and uncles I never knew existed. I even connected with my half-brother.

Now, I know the names of both my biological parents. I've seen pictures of my grandfather, affectionately called Grandpa Indian, and my great-grandfather, whose last name appears on Acoma Pueblo census rolls. I know where I come from. I am of Acoma Pueblo descent and a mix of European blood; I am colonized and colonizer. I know, too, that within me lies another wilderness, another story to follow. But this knowing has replaced most of the fear.

Caleb returns from placing the Rubber Boa safely in the trees. We retrieve our bicycles from the ditch and pedal slowly down the river road toward camp. Inside our camper awaits a stack of stories I'm revising for a collection titled *Salmon Weather*. These stories are like markers on a growth chart, cairns along a winding path, monuments to the person I was and am becoming. In them, I grapple with my identity as an adopted and Native person, navigating a space of unknowing.

In revising this collection, I've made a conscious decision to leave the stories as they were originally written. They reflect a particular moment in my journey, a time when much about my heritage remained shrouded in mystery. To alter them now, with my newfound knowledge, would be to erase that past self, to deny the authenticity of those earlier experiences. The stories I write going forward will undoubtedly reflect this new understanding, exploring different themes and concerns. But these essays remain untouched, a testament to the power of embracing uncertainty and the ever-evolving nature of identity.

I am a person unafraid to pick up snakes now—at least Rubber Boas and Garters. Who I'll be when I write the next story or poem begins here, with this newfound courage and a deeper understanding of my roots. Of who I am.

Along the Salmon River

We drive to the end of the road, Caleb and I, and park. A boat launch, gray and slick, eases gently into the clear water of the Salmon River. It has been raining, drizzling really, for the last two days. Everything is patinaed in gray: rocks, water, soil, sky. Even the cottonwood trees, vibrant in their golden death song, are a drabber version of themselves. We are walking west, beyond the road, the launch. Behind us change is coming; the sun is rising into skies clearing.

This trail is just the memory of a road, perhaps cut by hopeful miners, or scratched in by the Civilian Conservation Corps. I try to imagine how one might drive this road, but with every turn, my imagination drops a wheel off the edge and slips into the thick water below. This road has not been driven in years. Sixty, maybe seventy years. Only deer and the occasional elk walk stretches of it. The canyon is taking it back. In places brush has grown through the center of the trail and I must part it to stay on the path or grab its thick limb to hold me to the hillside; my feet proceed cautiously, one in front of the other. Here, a pine blackened by a years-ago fire has fallen, and I must straddle it to continue. For the rest of the day, I will carry ash between my thighs, my hands holding the memory of scorched bark.

I am not carrying the gun. I have only a small backpack and a trekking pole, the latter of which, I am both grateful for and frustrated with. In the narrowest parts it is a hindrance; I need both of my hands free to crawl up the hill or climb over a tree. Other times, after I stumble over a root, it saves me from falling, providing a third point of balance, a brace against the earth.

We have brought our two dogs. We are not expecting to see any deer and we feel guilty leaving them in the truck when we go out hiking, even now, even when we are hunting. They are quiet, good dogs, they stay between my partner and me. Still, I wonder if they will excite should they see a deer. A bear? Will a pine squirrel darting up a tree make them give chase and scare off any wandering wildlife? We have brought leashes, just in case.

The sun lights the hillside before us. Below us, the water has become an old mirror whose silver back has begun to wear away. There are no boats at the ramp, no boats in the water. Birds in the canyon this time of year are few. All we hear is the low and constant sound of the river wearing down its bank, a sound not unlike the one I hear laying my ear against my palm; it fills my head, it is the sound of life. We stop and my partner slowly brings his binoculars up and glasses the slope. He turns to me, and whispers, *It's a buck.*

Do you want it? I shake my head. It's still a quarter of a mile away and moving uphill. There is a ravine separating us, and who knows how much brush. I am not particularly quiet, nor am I fast. Nor am I willing to take the challenging shot that this might be: uphill, standing. I put the dogs on their leashes and bring them near as Caleb walks ahead. After he rounds a bend and I can no longer see him, I sit down. This will take some time.

For a while the dogs strain to watch him, then finally lie down. Their heads are an arrow of the same compass, and he is their North. I lean back against the slope and turn my attention to the opposite hillside. I am thinking of the black bear that we spooked yesterday afternoon. The bumbling, almost comic way that she waddled through the brush toward the ridgeline. How soft her muzzle looked through the binoculars, how cautious and yet unafraid she seemed when looking back at us. It's late autumn, soon she will go into hibernation. I wonder how many dens are on the north-facing slope before me.

This land that hips the Salmon River is largely open, swept. Wind, when it comes, is unabated, purposeful. It can rip a fire through this canyon in minutes, or, as it did last night, strip leaves from the deciduous trees and pull tears from the corners of my eyes. Before the bear, before the clearing afternoon, we had walked a trail through the rain into the Gospel Hump Wilderness, federally protected land on the north side of the Salmon. We just wanted to get out, to see the country in autumn, familiar as we were with it in spring. Once again, we were not expecting to see anything. We crossed the bridge and started up the Wind River trail. The hike began along a vast sandbar where two graves were marked with wooden crosses. We knew there were homesteads here. The land is covered with square skeletons of rock foundations and domestic with abandoned fruit trees. Five minutes into the walk, just as we passed under a barren apple tree, a buck deer came out of the brush and walked toward us. We froze. I would have taken that shot. He was close, calm, maybe rutting. I was not carrying the rifle. My partner turned to me; eyebrows furrowed. *Didn't you put bullets in this?* I shook my head and fished them from my pocket. The deer was only twenty yards away, watching us, so close I could throw a rock at him. Even when my partner chambered the bullet, the buck did not move, but bit instead at a gnat on his rump and looked back at us. Then, in a gesture like a truce flag rising, he flicked his tail, his black-tipped tail. Caleb lowered the raised rifle. *Mule deer*, he said. We were in a whitetail unit; both of us burst out laughing, a combination of praise for the buck's calmness and no small amount of relief, for despite our motives, neither of us takes pleasure in pulling the trigger. The buck strolled ten yards to a charred pine tree and stopped. He blinked twice at us, as if permitting us to leave.

We had been on this trail several months earlier. Early spring. There was still snow in the high mountain town of McCall where we live. This was our escape. The apple trees were just beginning to bloom. Lilacs, planted years ago from cuttings brought from who knows where, still held their deep purple and ambrosial promise. It had been a sunny day, the dogs were with us, unleashed. We carried only our packs, hastily made sandwiches, and liters of water. I was trailing behind but caught up when my partner came upon a stick of incense propped up with rocks in the middle of the trail. Then, a quarter mile later, another. They were smoldering, smoking, drifting a scent not belonging to this landscape. Bewildered, but curious, we kept moving up the trail, higher, until we came to a crest and a turn that would lead us down to the bridge that crosses the Wind River and takes us deeper into the Wilderness. At the top of the point, a man sat with a rifle. He was glassing the trail and slopes before him. We stopped and asked what he was hunting for. *Spring black bear. You guys?* Nothing, we were hunting for nothing, I told him. We were just out walking. As we moved down the trail in front of him, and for the rest of the hike, I felt the shadow of crosshairs on my back, the fine black lines that divide and target.

We tied our slickers around our waists and walked another twenty minutes down the trail, stopping short of the site where we had seen the bear hunter the year before. Going back, we leave the trail and walk along the easy edge of the river, where we come across another grave. "Buck Hamel" is carved into a wooden cross, with "Man's Best Friend," written beneath. Beside the grave, a lilac, stunted by a recent fire, blooms out of season. I am astonished by the contradictions that fill the Salmon River canyon and I recognize myself as one of them. The weight of the gun was heavy on my shoulder.

I stretch and bring myself back to the morning. I can see my partner nearing the ravine. I look to the hillside and can see three deer now.

Does? Bucks? I cannot tell, only that they are moving slowly uphill, as deer will do of a morning, after they have taken their drink, grazing as they move toward afternoon beds. Their bodies are sunlit and tawny, they blend into the dying grass. Bedded, they will be difficult to see, almost impossible, but here, with the steepness and curve of the canyon they are beautifully and dangerously contrasted against the sky.

As my partner's head clears the horizon the smallest deer jumps. The other two deer have spotted him, but don't run. All three take a few steps back, moving around the edge of the hill, stepping out of my view. Animals here, past the road's end, are used to the comings and goings of people on the river, but they don't have much pressure on the land. My partner is on the hill now, crouching, then, I assume crawling, looking not unlike yesterday's bear.

The damp air, like a freshly dug hole; it's crisp and clean when it reaches my nose, but there is a rot at the base of it. It is coming on stronger each day we are here. It is leaves, berries, and the yellow-bronze needle of larch slowly decomposing, composting. The earth exhaling her summer breath before the winter freeze. In the leafless tree in front of me, or maybe from across the river, an owl hoots. The question bounces back and forth across the canyon walls and settles onto the water. I have always loved this unsettling sound, even though Pima friends once told me that an owl is a harbinger of death. I lean back against the hillside and wait, the cool, damp earth finally penetrating my thick trousers and settling into the silk leggings I wear beneath.

I shiver despite the sun that glints off the river promising short sleeves by noon. I know I will not be warm until I start hiking again. My nose drips, and I keep wiping it with the back of my gloved hand, not wanting to sniff, wanting to stay quiet. My eyes fall to the river, and I follow it until it turns north. The Salmon is one of the longest undammed rivers in the lower forty-eight. There are no manmade barriers between here and the river's thin beginning, nearly three hundred miles away in the mountains above Stanley, Idaho. I fling my heart upstream like a rock skipping, and wonder if it could make it all the way to the headwaters, or only to the other side. I am in love with this Salmon River country. The steep slopes, wind-swept trees, the deer and elk—it's where I feel most myself, most free. Yet the land holds a fierce beauty, a danger in its summer heat. Even those who share my love for it could crush my spirit with their conflicting desires.

I want to protect this place, as I do anything I love, to shield the life it cradles. But love is a complex thing. This isn't the first time I've wrestled with the act of taking a life to sustain my own. It's not the first time we've walked these hills, hoping not to see our prey, only to shatter the silence with a shot. And I know, as the echo fades, it won't be the last.

The dog's strain against their leads. One wants to go toward the sound and the other wants to go back to the truck. I calm them both before I rise, wipe the dew from my trousers, and reach for my trekking pole. We wait a moment, listen for a second shot, and when none comes, start moving quickly along the trail. Upstream I hear the high-pitched wail of a jet boat and watch it slide down the middle of the Salmon, unzipping the water with its wake. This I can feel in my chest. This is what I will have to put aside when I reach Caleb and the buck. I listen for the owl and hear only a raven.

A Story About a South Fork Salmon River Logging Road and What it Means to be a Good Ancestor

This is the story of a river, a road, and a fish.

The river is the South Fork of the Salmon. More specifically, the stretch of the South Fork of the Salmon River that begins near the summit until it joins the Sesech River beneath my favorite bridge, a bridge that curves to hug the river, that curves like a comma asking drivers to pause as they cross, to pause and look into the water below, to look as if there are answers in the water, because there are. But this bridge is not on the road that this story is interested in, but the road and the bridge and the fish that swim in the river are all on the way to the place where our story begins.

The trail, like the river, like the fish, pre-date white settlement, yet it was formed by human feet. It is kept up now by hooves and paws and on a day in late May, the tread of my own soles, following the tread of my partner, who has promised me wonder. On this day, the hillside is golden with balsamroot arrowleaf. I have known many flowers, but the balsamroot, to my knowing, is most companionable. Iris of gold, pupil of earth. I am never alone when walking among them, each petaled eye watching my step, greeting me from beside the trail, giving me glimpses into the soil that is the soul of all beings. Looking now into those brown eyes, I see ancestors, human and greater than, every being whose bone and ash fed the balsamroots growth, fed the others that grow here, too, fed the deer whose body feeds my own. Once, before I stopped picking flowers, I tucked a stem behind my ear and for a moment, gained another sight, in that moment, seeing through the soil-colored and gilded eye, I saw what I think I can call grace. For a moment, I knew what was meant by the words, " Consider the lilies, how they grow: They do not toil, nor do they spin."

But this morning, the one of our story, the one after I stopped picking flowers, choosing instead to hold them with my eyes, sometimes a lens, let them grow and flourish to be breakfast for deer, or bee, or just to remain in poetry as the place where sunrises are born, this morning I merely greeted them as I toiled up the steep trail, the very old trail, with my dogs, my man, and the song of robins above me and somewhere, over the ridge and the sound of river, the low groan of what I thought may be a tractor.

To know the landscape of the South Fork of the Salmon River, raise your hands to heart height, palms down, and lace your fingers together until right knuckles meet left. Here, the river winds through. It is still cutting the canyon that holds it. And the webs between fingers are drainages. We can name a few now, though we know they have had many names, today we will call them Buckhorn and Camp and Phoebe and Nasty. And as you imagine the landscape of your hands as the state of Idaho, the state that holds the South Fork of the Salmon River, you will see how steep your fingers have become, what a travail it may be to get to the back of your hand, but what a gift the summit will be when you reach it. The view notwithstanding, the back of your hand becomes a hopeful place, an easier walk. This is where we are headed, the back of your hand that is the ridgeline, though, for the sake of our story and the stories yet to come, let's not name this drainage we walk, nor this creek. Names can be important and I hope you'll forgive my lie of omission, but trails like the one we are taking to the top of this ridge are best left unnamed, just as some wishes are left unspoken if you want them to come true.

The day is cool. It will rain. This, Caleb, a fish biologist, tells me is Salmon Weather. And yes, there are Salmon in the South Fork of the Salmon River. And they are part of this story of river, road, and fish. But let's say they are more than just Salmon. In this story, they represent all the fish in the river, from Steelhead to Sculpin, to Lamprey. And the weather matters greatly to this story, particularly that it is Salmon Weather because Salmon Weather means rain and rain means that from the top of the ridgeline we see in your hands, water will flow down, down, down into the creek or the Sesech and down into the South Fork of the Salmon River which goes down to the main Salmon itself and is passing now, not far from here, in the Snake River which becomes the Columbia and then the Pacific and somewhere in that water, right now, Summer Chinook are carrying food for Balsamroot and Black Bear, and the Ponderosa Pine that, too, will become part of our story. They are carrying food and their own story as they make their way upstream, a travail not like the simple walk up the drainage of our hands, but one that overcomes dams, fights current, and jumps falls to come to the headwaters, where our story and the river began, Big Creek Summit. Spring rain, spring snow, runoff, water. The banks of the creeks fill, even if only slightly, and they rise the Sesech and the South Fork of the Salmon and the main and so on down the line. And in the times before the dams, the waters naturally rose for Salmon to swim through boulders and falls, and to make their way up thin streams and wrist-like tributaries to that place, holds the eggs of Salmon who will soon hatch and who will grow and grow and eventually ride the spring waters down and down, passing us, passing each other, and so passing their story on to a new generation.

There is something else about the rain. When it falls, as soon it will, on the ridge above the drainage where we hike this early May morning, it will loosen the soil. Snow knows to do this too. And that soil will let go, and it will roll down the hillside, past Arrowleaf and Ponderosa, to a road. And that road is where this story might have stopped. Because in this landscape, and in this story, the road begins to complicate and change things; like the dams, it begins to upset the natural order or downward movement. Disrupts a process the river and fish depend upon. Here, on this road, the rolling bits of earth and water would stop. Like a camera stills life with a photograph. But it is much more complicated than a photo. And yet, it is a little like pausing life. Because those hillsides have always offered something to the river, from bits of soil to fallen Ponderosa, this downward movement, at the earth's own pace, is a necessary continuation of life.

The road was important once, too. It was part of a maze of roads cut into the fingers of the hillside, zigzagging back and forth, swaying as if dancing, and taking each tree it came to as a partner, shaking the dress of limbs until the final dip, from a feller or saw, a dip from which the coniferous dancer never recovered. It was a dance of industry and growth. The 1950s. The pride of lumberjacks who, I know, loved the South Fork of the Salmon River, loved these hills and Arrowleaf and pines as much as I do. As much as the Nimiipuu and the Tukadeka whose cambium peels are scars, too. Love, we can agree, is as hard to define as Idaho itself. And perhaps, both are best that way. But then something happened. Something changed. Perhaps our love.

Perhaps we found we could love or need a thing too much. And so hundreds of miles were cut into hills, thousands of trees were cut into board feet, and certain slopes of the South Fork became as bare as the back of your hands. And when the big machines rolled away, when many of the old trees were gone and the lumberjacks moved on, the stumps that thrust from the earth became fists or tombstones with epitaphs in circles of circles containing old songs, bird songs, containing thunderstorms, holding the story of the South Fork and the Salmon River in their rings.

I have seen the South Fork before the roads. In a black and white photograph found after our hike, buried in archives that I stumbled upon almost as if by accident, but perhaps it was providence, for here is a haunting coincidence. The photo taken in 1904, more than a hundred years old, was taken from the same trail where I followed the tread of my partner, the hooves, and paws, and the footsteps of ancestors. Not just from the same trail, but the same *exact* place. R.E. Benedict, the photographer, stood where I stood, but some 107 years earlier. There was no road into the South Fork then, no gentle curve of bridge, no signs at creek crossings, no lookouts on the peaks. There were no dams on the Snake. Idaho had been a state for only 15 years. And the US Forest Service would not be the Forest Service for another year. But Teddy and Pinchot had the wheels turning. And the photograph was taken by a man sent to scout for potential forest reserves. The label on the photo: BULL PINE YELLOW PINE, is not a place, but a resource. Food for a growing nation. The photographer and his Horses or Mules or Horses and Mules, his gear, weighty and cumbersome, took this old trail up and up and set up his equipment first east, then west. I wonder what the trees heard in that moment. Did the camera shutter echo through the canyon; did the Horses and Mules flinch? Did the Deer? Did the Elk or Flicker or Salmon? Was there a notion in that shutter of what was to come? What does grace sound like? Did it sound like this?

And so began a new story for the South Fork of the Salmon. One that began with, among other things, a photograph.

Before I knew of the man and his camera, before the archives and the rain that was coming, the rain that brought us to this pause in the road, I made pictures of my own. First east, then west. It was an outcropping of rock, a prominence, a place of view and I climbed atop it and paused because sometimes, because anymore, I am stilled by beauty. I am brought to awe. Sometimes to tears. Tears that confuse me as much as they comfort me, for they seem not to know the difference between *beauty-joy* and *beauty-pain*, so sometimes I hoard the emotion in a photograph. I collect the beauty into a picture that I pour out to friends, to myself, over and over again when solace seems so hard to find. When I need to remind myself that there are places where, despite roads and logging, despite conflicts and catastrophes, despite the longing of a river for her fish, the Lodgepole for their first names, and despite what would come after the flinch of that first shutter, perhaps the very first shutter to ever close on the slopes, on the steep fingers that feed water and sediment and boulders and seed into the South Fork of the Salmon River, there is a place that I can turn to, even only if in a photograph, where I stand on the edge of hope. And perhaps it is the immutability of the photograph, that stasis, that held beauty, that I need in order to believe in something as difficult as hope. Is this what is meant by faith? Look to the Arrowleaf who neither toil nor spin.

There is something else about photographs, about looking into places where we can imagine. Something Wallace Stegner wrote in his *Wilderness Letter*, "Something will have gone out of us as a people if we ever let the remaining wilderness be destroyed ... We simply need that wild country available to us, even if we never do more than drive to its edge and look in." He called it a geography of hope and perhaps Benedict did, too. And perhaps the loggers and the miners and the homesteaders that came in and pushed out the Tukedeka, Nimiipuu, Salmon, Wolves, Grizzly, and how many others who had a different name or no name, a different story or no story at all for this place, also saw something that looked, to them, like hope.

Then again, maybe hope as a landscape only exists within privilege and power. Is only afforded to some to those for whom the geography is not also within them. For the privileged, hope may be the short view, like the photograph that can hold only so much, that can show only a bit of an entire landscape. For I believe that wilderness to Native people, native fishes, and even some poets is not so easily labeled. Is not seen as commodity. Is not wilderness at all—is life. Is home. Maybe like the hands you used to make the landscape of the South Fork, maybe there is nothing but wilderness, so nothing but home, and knowing this means that we, too, are part of the landscape and that what had been inflicted, what was in the 1940s and 50s, about to be inflicted would cause Native people and beings to gain an emotion they hadn't yet needed, to lose what was home in the name of another's hope.

I believe that those who came after Benedict, the loggers, the CCC workers, the miners, and those who would homestead, thought their presence and their work was good. I like to believe they took pride in their work. They truly believed they were building a good future for their children. I like to think that whoever drove the tractor that made the road that I am telling you about, told a story of progress and industry to children who would look with pride at their father trusting that yes, the trees would regrow, yes this land of plenty would always be, and yes they were fair to those who had first called this place home. And though now we know differently, believing this story helps me believe the next one. The one I am trying to tell. The one that says we are capable of a great many things including recognizing our mistakes, questioning our choices, and making new stories.

Come back with me now to the pause of the rain on the road. The pause is the problem. For the rain that once flowed down or moved around the hillside now gathers. Pools. Makes runnels that follow a different path to the river. Now that natural downward flow is disrupted and the road becomes a rivulet. Sometimes it slides, and though slides had happened before in the South Fork (steep country like this is bound to sluff), the slides carry an unnatural amount of dirt and rock to the river. And in the years following the logging, there were fewer trees left to hold the land, to shade and feed plants whose roots, like ours, can give stability. And so into the river who was already missing Salmon, dams in the Snake and Columbia blocking their return, came large amounts of sediment. Not that sediment is always bad. Mussels love it. Sculpin, too. But this amount meant additional work for Salmon. Meant destruction of the redds where they lay their eggs, where their fry are hatched. And here is where I want to be careful, and here is where I want to tell you that with grace and deep knowledge, my partner, the fisheries biologist, Caleb, stood on a ridgeline of a morning in May and in details that I cannot remember, some I cannot understand, explained years of research that shows the effects that these zigzagging roads had on a species that was already, and is still, struggling. And just as the lines are many across the slopes of your hands, so were the roads. More road than tree. More erosion than retention. More sediment than a river can move.

Before the photograph, I had not known the South Fork without the logging roads. I can recall first glimpses, my finger pointing to the Z's on the slopes, and Caleb repeating, "It doesn't *go* anywhere. It's a logging road," and not understanding fully why a road would be built to nowhere. And in those early years, when I still hunted the steep canyons for deer, the roads were a way in. Dense and steep as the country is, the roads, or what was left of them, were easy walking. But even as some roads had been kept open, others had been closed or forgotten, and walking them (though easier than a straight scramble up) meant climbing over fallen trees, squeezing through Ceanothus, meant sometimes seeing that which the loggers had left behind. Of the hundreds of miles I have walked in the South Fork, many of them have been on these logging roads, or logging roads that became trails.

It took some time, as love often does, to see that the roads, though convenient, had done something else. Had left behind a permanent change on the landscape. And in the way the beings could be on the landscape. Now the side-by-side roars. The mountain bikes hoorah over passes. Dirt bikes rev from peak to peak. And often still, the hooves and paws leave their mark on these trails. How much easier it must be to move quickly up a cleared switchback, yet how much more vulnerable it must also make one. What I am trying to say is I fell in love with the South Fork, despite its scarred hillsides. In fact, I never imagined the South Fork any other way than roaded, than scarred. This was my story of the South Fork, and, I thought, that despite what Caleb's research was finding, this is how it would always be. And so long as it would stay the same, by which I think that I meant so long as it didn't become developed, that no more roads were built, that no dams were ever constructed on it, that we took proactive steps to prevent further harm, that I would be ok with this story. Even happy with the way things were on the South Fork. And I could hope that somewhere down river something could change to bring more Salmon back, the roads that were closed would stay closed and the Ceanothus might grow over them and cover our scars. But the land could never fully erase the cuts we'd made as roads into the hillside. "Wisdom," Stegner writes, "is knowing what you have to accept." What I didn't know was this was not the story of the South Fork I had to accept. What I didn't know was that the reason Caleb had brought me to this old trail, this "Indian Trail" (as it is written on the old maps) was that a new story was happening on the land. A restoration, a re-storyation, had begun.

The story of the South Fork, up to this point, could be the story of many places in the west. Settlers moved in; Natives were pushed out. What was feared—from Wolves and Grizzlies to Nez Perce and Tukedeka—were killed or removed. Manifest Destiny was invoked, and trees and rivers and deer and land were commodified and called resources. A certain amount of greed settled in so what once seemed bountiful, innumerable, was taken and taken by saw or gun, by dredge or drill, by one person, by companies, by government entities created to preserve the place, and then the land was either colonized or abandoned. In the areas labeled "public," plans were written, and promises about caring for the land and serving the people were made, then sometimes realized. In the areas abandoned by industry, a pall settled in. Sometimes the land was seen as used up or use-less. Lakes were labeled barren because they produced no fish— the rivers were reduced to reservoirs that allowed no Salmon, no rich ocean nutrient, and so became thick with algae and without floods could no longer clean themselves. And this says nothing of the people. Particularly Native people who, as resilient as the landscape can be when it is not dismantled and permanently scarred, are, alongside Salmon, trying to, despite all the obstacles, return home. To awaken first languages. Return to natal waters, to a cultural home dependent on the landscape as familiar as the back of their hand. And when looked at in this way, it sometimes becomes so large as to seem impossible. To seem immutable or at least as if things are only getting worse. How can we ever imagine anything different if this same story of the west is told over and over again, in both action and words?

I forgot to mention the Clarkia that lined the steep trail. Such a deep purple and more than I have ever seen. I forgot the Ponderosa that stood alone on the hillside. A massive being maybe three stories tall. I have not known many larger, for most of the old trees, as we've learned, are gone, and even as this one is arrow straight and prime for the mill, it stands still, and that afternoon we sat with our backs against it and ate our lunches looking west. Our old dog, Carhartt, fell asleep among the Lodgepole's fallen needles. Cisco wagged, his eyes trained on some distant horizon. Above us, a family of Flickers was being raised and I wondered just how many families had known this tree. I closed my eyes and tried to see all the tree had seen. Nimiipuu and Tukeda, Wolves and Grizzly, roadless and roaded, Benedict and now me. There were no doubt nutrients from the Pacific, delivered in spent Salmon bodies, shat by Eagles and Turkey Vultures had fed its heart wood. And though this tree bore witness to logging, mines, and so many roads it did not witness the full extent of the destruction that could have been, it. There on that hillside, I found comfort in that, because whatever it is—hope, or just the need to see an unaltered landscape—can still be found here.

When the rain finally came, it fell with a fervor. As if each drop had a job to do, and was being deployed with a singular focus. The clouds threw the rain down and despite our attempt to shelter beneath a tree, the rain found us, too, and in no time all that was protected with coat and hat became cold and wet. Rain dripped from the whiskers of the dogs, from the brims of our hats. Rain ran like tears on our cheeks. Rain trickled like a chill down the spine. The old dog stood in the rain as if to challenge it. The younger dog nosed his way beneath bent legs as if never in his canine lineage were dogs and water to meet. And me, I thought of the water that was gathering in the river, gathering on the slope, water that would make its way to the roots of the old lodgepole, of the arrowleaf, that would gather and roll down the hillside, down and down to the road. But this time the water would not stop, not collect on the road. This rain would be the first to fall on what *was* the road and that was the reason that Caleb had brought me on this spring hike, to watch the water run all the way down.

When the storm passed, as storms in this part of the Salmon River Mountains quickly do, I found the source of the early sound of an engine. An orange excavator. We shed our wet coats as the dogs shook water from their own and Caleb motioned me forward.

When Caleb first spoke the word "obliteration," I flinched. It sounded like destruction, and destruction is something I fear for the South Fork. Then I saw its result, and indeed, it looked like destruction. Downed trees and upturned earth. The ground opened and mounded. But this destruction, this obliteration, was different. In all this glorious landscape, this is what we had come to see. The earth turned upside down. The big orange excavator working its way backward, down the ridgeline, down the old road bed whose compacted soil it tears up as it moves. From above and below that 70-year-old roadbed the toothed scoop pulled earth and rocks. The machine pulled trees and transplanted them in the now gone road, which I have learned, take root more often than not.

Moving at about six feet an hour, the excavator and its single driver undo time. Mend a tear. Pull the earth back together like the seams of a wound. And for a moment, it is as if we are watching history undo. And when the excavator reaches the river, it will be driven to the top of another nowhere-going road and the obliteration will begin again. And again, until hundreds of miles of roads are obliterated from this rugged and beautiful landscape, from this South Fork country.

When we reach the place where the Indian trail meets the road that is no longer a road, I am overcome by the promising smell of fresh earth. Soon, a woman will walk past, a canvas bag over her shoulder filled with seeds, native seed mix, seeds of Yarrow and Bunchgrass. She will scatter this seed while others transplant smaller bushes, into newly uncompacted soil that was only hours earlier, road. She will follow the excavator as it leaves a slope where a shelf had been. And the irony of the Indian trail meeting the road, the native seed planted in the uncompacted soil, the tribe and the government coming together, Benedict's photo and Stegner's story of hope meeting mine, the healing of wounds, or maybe what looks like a metaphor for the beginning of healing between ancestors new and old, is not lost on me.

After the woman with her seeds and the workers with their shovels leave the first tracks, the land will be left to itself. The sound of the heavy equipment that has brought destruction and grace will reside only in the rings of the Ponderosa. The rain that fell, the rain that gave us pause and chill, the rain that came as if it had a job to do, will soak into the soil that is the soul of all things in the South Fork of the Salmon River. Will make its way to seed, to root, and I will feel something like I felt the first time I saw the South Fork, something like I felt when I saw the upturned earth, something like I hadn't imagined was possible. I will feel something like love, something like hope. And what gives me the most hope in this story has less to do with what this unroading will do for the fish and the river, though that is very important, too. This hope I feel welling, like my pain beauty tears, is the hope for my own species, for humankind. Because in the plan that created this change, the forest plan, the plan of land managers, was a plan future thinking, a story written by those who will be seen as good ancestors even as they will never live to see the full outcome of their work. For though it will take half a century or more for the wound to heal, it will. And there is a chance that another woman, a century after my passing, as in love as I am with the South Fork of the Salmon River, will, of a May morning, walk up what she assumes is a game trail. She will follow the tracks of Wolves and Bear, the heart-shaped hoof prints of Deer, and the musk of Elk. She will look into the eyes of the Arrowleaf not knowing all the ancestors looking back at her. She will, I hope, hear the ghosts of others, of me, that ask her to stop at a certain precipice and look, first west, then east. To pause near the base of a Ponderosa that may by then be only a snag, a ghost itself, still stalwart and knowing, and lean against it and stare upon a landscape unroaded. And what she will see is what some have called *resource*, some have called *preserve*, some have called *wilderness*, and still others call home. What she will see is not an ideal or metaphor, not a geography or even a healing. What she will see is the South Fork as it is meant to be, as it was celebrated by the land's first people, as the definition of awe. And compelled then by beauty and not the fear of losing it, she will speak to the ghosts of good ancestors. She will search for the words, as I did on that May morning, and they will be simple, and they will be timeless, and they will be welcome, and those words will be *Thank you.*

Epilogue

By spring of 2024, 300 miles of road have been obliterated in the South Fork of the Salmon River. 200 more are scheduled for obliteration.

Though it is too soon to tell the effect these actions will have on the streams, tributaries, and fishes below, we can look to old data, from the hundreds of miles of decommissioned roads on the Payette National Forest, the Nez Perce Clearwater National Forest, and others and know that the work is not in vain. It's important to note, too, that healing the land, at least in the South Fork, is not unlike healing a body. Groups once at odds, both federal and local, tribal and non, came together to heal a landscape, remove a road, support a river, and save her fish. There are a lot of words for this kind of action from *collaboration* to *community*, but whatever you call it, know that names are mutable as are definitions of words. Like love, but maybe more like the definition of hope. We are, as humans, capable of a great many things. "The wounds men make in the earth do not quickly heal," writes Stegner. "Still they are only wounds; they are absolutely mortal. Better a wounded wilderness than none at all."

Lace your fingers together one more time for another look at the South Fork of the Salmon River; perhaps you can see it a little more clearly now. The drainages between your fingers. The steepness of the ridges. Imagine it as it can be in five years, in fifty years, and see the river as it flows between your fingers, where the round of your knuckles meets. The river has been carving the canyon of the South Fork of the Salmon River for millions of years. Its story begins in the rock and soil buried beneath mussel beds and rainstorms, cobble, and time. You can see it, or start to if you roll your palms upward. Look how they form something like a basin, look at how they seem to be giving something away, look at the life that runs in the lines. It's there, there is the answer, the one I told you was in the river beneath the bridge that curves over a confluence. There is what it takes to make a new story. This is where the future of the South Fork, the Salmon that is all fish, the West, and the future of our predecessors lives. This is the true geography of hope. Right where it should be, right there in your hands.

Coyote Story

Autumn, Beartooth Front Country. The sky and landscape are buckskin and blue. I am driving my Ford pickup down the roads that encircle the ranch I am living on, caretaking. Though little work other than keeping a fire going and feeding the owner's horses is required. I am an hour from the nearest town. From almost anywhere on the ranch, I see no neighbors. I am out driving just to be out, to be looking across the vast distances that have always filled me. This is a land devoid of structures. Of obvious human intervention. Here, I can imagine. I can dream without intrusion of even a fence line. And those dreams are never lonesome things, they are filled with stories. Memory. The call of meadowlark. The huff of a doe muley. The song of coyote. All my insides find home here and resonate back to me in the enormity of a southern Montana prairie.

I come up over a small rise, and, in the distance, something jumps. Once, then again. An awkward jump. Almost sideways. Almost a pounce. At first, I think I am seeing a rabbit. Perhaps a fox. But the color is wrong. The size. I press down the brake and reach for my binoculars, bring them to my eyes. As I turn the thumbwheel, a brown coyote comes into focus. She throws her head back as if tugging. Pulling against some force that holds her in place, yet I cannot see what. I lift my foot from the brake and roll forward.

I don't know when I realize the coyote's left ankle is caught between two horseshoe-shaped jaws of a dull silver trap. I walk from the truck to the coyote. Each step in the reddish-brown soil raises puffs of dirt around my feet. As I grow near, I realize how much like my own dog, Katie, this coyote is. The same size, the same amber eyes. Then I see the blood in the soil. The swelling and rawness of an ankle chewed. The coyote has dug at the trap with her free forepaw. Her mouth—a mud of blood and froth. As I draw closer, the coyote begins to growl, to bear her front teeth.

I walk a circle around the trapped animal. I look for ways to spring the trap, but traps such as these are not something with which I am familiar. My breath and words stick when I talk to the coyote. Only platitudes escape. I look toward the passenger window of my blue truck. From inside, I can see my dog Katie looking out at me. Her eyes begged the question: What are you going to do? One dog in my truck who needs my protection and one at my feet who inherently knows I am not to be trusted.

The sky on that day was the color of the paper on which I wrote this story. Not white, not gray. Caught in the middle somewhere. The color of possibility here, but not when enshrouding the gruesome scene unfolding on the prairie. The sky that day held certainties. The story for the coyote could have only one ending. Winter was coming; there was no doubt about that. The clouds spit and its drops were cold and sharp against my face.

I keep recalling that day. I keep coming back to the coyote story not because I think I could have done anything different; the fate of the coyote was set in motion when the first white people came west, and it was handed down through the men and myths that made the man from the town of Bridger set the trap on that barren hillside, place a bit of ground beef around it, and yawn open that metal mouth. I would never meet that man, but he would find my reply to the question of his bait. He would, in the prints I left in the dirt, in the metal I destroyed with a maul, know my anger. Yet I was the one guilty of trespass. The law protected his right to trap. To mangle the leg of the coyote, but not to let her suffer, bleed, and starve for hours, days. My only witness was the prairie. I keep coming back to the coyote story because I forget how it ends for me. There are so many possibilities but writing it here will set us both straight.

And I keep coming back to the coyote because I work in metaphor. Symbol. I see patterns. I find story. The first story is of the coyote and me. The next belongs to those I called in the hope that we might save the coyote. The county vet, who would later corner me in my barn when he came over to float my mare's teeth, denied help. My friend Ron, from a thousand miles away, assured me there was nothing else I could do. The third story died with my dog Katie, who I am certain consisted entirely of story. She watched intently that day through the closed window. I do not pretend to know how she translated what she saw, but I am certain that when I got back in the truck, the cursory sniff she gave was not to catch a scent of her wild cousin but to be certain it was I who sat beside her and drove us back to the house. I left the coyote as I found her and drove Katie home to put her in my bedroom. I could not bear for her to witness what would happen next.

Writing teachers have encouraged me not to anthropomorphize nature, while elders tell me that we, nature and I, are the same. I tend to write on the side of elders. I believe that trees exhibit emotion, and I am haunted by a young doe, whether sister or mate, that walked around the corpse of a newly shot buck, unable to leave his side out of a devotion I fully understand. And the buck's meat wasn't filled with the bitter taste of regret but filled me with a desire to live a life worthy of its wild sustenance.

Yet another story. A metaphor. A reminder of how, for an hour after my husband had drowned, I lay beside him, holding him, unwilling to let his body be taken from me. To be carried off not for sustenance, but autopsy. Cremation. We die so many times in one life. A certain sky that day, too. I did not anthropomorphize the river that carried his last breath away with so much spring runoff. I did not hope that it would somehow consider me and my pain as it did. Though now that I am older, now that I have known twenty more years of rivers, I might tell you they are the most abiding, always returning what they take. Somewhere, off the gulf where the spring runoff finally met with the sea, I believe I retrieved my husband's breaths and made them mine.

Older now, twenty or more years, I come back to the coyote story. And I have known some coyotes since, both those taught to me in traditional stories and those who met me in the wild, rearing dens of pups a fifteen-minute walk from where I now live. Katie was old when she met those coyote parents. We were jogging. They came out from the brush and ran alongside us. It all happened so quickly that I still don't know if it was providence or omen. They did not try to bite either of my dogs. They only paralleled us in the brush and barked as if ushering us off. They were protecting their kin. We had trespassed. The dogs, I will not say, dwelled on that. But I did. Being human in the West, in the moderately wild places I live in, *is* a threat, no matter how kindly and carefully I walk. The deer will tell you that. The coyote. In the spring, when I am hiking and not hunting, I tell the animals who stop to gaze at me as I gaze back in adoration that I am not to be trusted. I am two people. I will be seeking a different sustenance in a few months. I try to live in a way so as to deserve that.

Along the Salmon River, in spring, in a place where the previous fall I hunted deer, I once met a young buck and doe. As if I were joking, for I thought I was, I told Caleb to stop the truck and ready the camera; I was going to get out and pet them. I stepped out of the truck and walked up to the pair. In no time, I was scratching them behind the ears, and they were gently nudging me with their heads. Trying to play.

The picture Caleb took shows an undeniable happiness. Joy. My arm around the buck, the doe with her nose to my cheek. Would the deer, anthropomorphized, title this picture *Forgiven*? My practice of hunting has not changed. Nor of praying that the meat I take is ingested by someone who lives a life well enough to deserve it. But who's to judge guilt or innocence? "I contain multitudes," Whitman writes.

I have known other coyotes as well, albeit from a distance. Along roadsides, through scat, at night in song, and this winter, on the eve of my forty-eighth birthday, from a rock above the San Juan River near Bluff, Utah. To my right, hundreds of paintings and peckings left by thousands of years of visitors to this place. To my left, Navajo land. It was late December, but the sun was strong. Caleb and I, lizard-like, stretched out on the warm rocks and watched as the water rolled by like hammered silver. First, a foursome of ducks came floating along on the current. When they were startled, splashed, and flew off downriver, we spotted the source of their fear: a coyote wandering out of the thick, invasive tamarisk. Then another. And behind them a mostly black Angus ambled out, a yellow tag punched in her left ear. They all walked to the edge of the San Juan and drank together. My dogs watched with quiet intention. The coyotes did not notice us, or if they did, they didn't care. They had the river on their side. I raised my camera and took a picture of the threesome, and then, as if called, all three turned and walked back into that dense brush. The picture, no matter how you look at it, shows three coyotes.

Native stories about coyote are about a trickster. Mocking stories. Moral stories. Coyote made human. Anthropomorphic. In other stories, Coyote is a protector. His antics are a way to keep the other animals safe. We don't tell Coyote stories in summer, so I will not go on, but you should know that, at least in my grandfather's stories, magic surrounds Coyote. Is there a reverse process for anthropomorphizing? Do animals give animal traits to humans in an effort to live better? To understand us? Would the coyotes on the riverbank tell stories about the humans lounging on the rock? What would the moral or lesson be? Would the coyote see the two people I am? Native elders would say Coyote and human are one.

I think often about the two people I am. Is that all of me there is? Can I discern one from the other, or have I gotten too close? A friend once asked how it was that I pulled the silver trigger of my .30-06 when it was pointed at the right shoulder of a cow elk on an early winter slope. Something else took over, I told her. I had clicked the safety off and then back on a dozen or more times. My finger moved as delicately past the trigger guard as it does when tracing the bone of my lover's jaw. I am two people. The other one pulled the trigger. The one who writes on this sky the color of month-old snow pushes the "U" key on this keyboard with her trigger finger. Draws it to my lips to say *shhh* when the dogs bark at the sight of a bear and her cubs. Maybe within me are two survivors. One that kills and one that cleans up.

There is a metaphor for my life in the river story. The one about the coyote and the cow. It is about my biological parents. One Acoma, one European. This is the story I was told. The story of me. I am of two people. Colonized and colonizer. I am of two continents. Maybe more. How do I bring them together? How do I set them free?

The story of the coyote in the trap is the one I come back to as I write about Native women. How the law protects the trapper. Allows sufferings. The removal of pests. Not more than an hour's walk from where the coyote was trapped is the Crow reservation. A wild horse refuge. Everywhere there is story. Ice caves. Native women have been disappearing by the thousands. There is no record of this in federal courts or by police authorities off the reservation. The highest number of disappearing women occurs near man camps. Those temporary lodgings set up for oil field workers in places such as Williston, North Dakota. Under white skies. The county vet would back me into a corner in the barn and say that now that my husband was dead he could help me, could take care of me. I hid in the basement when he came to my house, my right finger to my lips asking the dogs to shush. I did not want to disappear. My grandfather prayed for all our relations.

Is mine the narrative of the West? In this story I am Crazy Horse; in others I am Columbus. Which one, my friend asks me, pulls the trigger? How do you know who to trust?

I keep coming back to the coyote story because I shot the coyote. Twice. The first time I tried, I stepped out of my truck with a .40 caliber Smith and Wesson handgun in my right hand. I carried it against the flesh of my right thigh. When I got close to the coyote and the coyote paused, I raised the gun. I am trained in firearms. Was captain of the pistol team in college. I am of two countries, one colonized and one colonizer. I don't know which one bought the gun I raised. I was close enough not to need to look through the sights. I cupped my left hand under my right. Pointed it at the dog. For that is what she is in the end. A dog. My Katie was in the truck waiting. I've known no truer friend.

Older now, I come back to the coyote story. I have killed deer and elk since then. I write about the Native experience. About Native women's bodies. I went to a college built on Nez Perce lands and colonial ideals. I bonded with white mentors and argued with white men who told me the land was not stolen, and that the Indian was conquered. I am called *squaw* by those who think that word can control me. I am asked if I am Mexican or, once, Greek. "What's your bloodline?" I was asked. As if a horse. We are the animals, elders say. We are many people in one. It was a dog. We should not anthropomorphize. Show, they kept telling me with my poems, don't tell. I cannot show you; I must tell you the story of the woman who shot the coyote. Twice.

I could not kill it, you see. Not with the pistol. My right hand started to tremble. Eyes amber like my Katie's. I drove the miles back to the ranch house, left Katie inside my room, and took my .30-06 from the wall. The .30-06 I would use, years later, to kill the pregnant cow elk. The same rifle I bought for my late husband the Christmas before he died. I drove the bumpy road back past the place where I first spotted the animal. Past my innocence, my naivete. I parked twenty yards from the coyote and cut the engine. I got out and did not close the door. I just lay my breasts against the warmth of the hood and placed the coyote's head in the fine crosshairs of my rifle, my finger slid past the trigger guard to the trigger, and I pulled it. Something else took over.

But my shot was hasty and ill-placed and hit the coyote in the back end, blowing apart her hind leg and rendering her motionless, but alive. I keep coming back to the coyote story to try to find out who it was that tossed the rifle back into the pickup and pulled out the pistol, crossed the short distance between us, lay the muzzle of the .40 to the soft spot of hair beneath the coyote's left ear and fired.

I am two people. One who kills. One who cleans up.

Perhaps there are more. Countless others. Like the river that carried my husband's breath back to me and also carried the breaths of all the lives it claimed. We are in and of the world, the elders tell me. I contain multitudes. I drank the river that came from my husband's mouth and carried on my hands the blood of coyote and elk. I can smell the breath still of the county vet and Katie's paws after she ran through grass.

Every death is a loss, every memory a birth. How many times can we die in one life and still breathe? I come back to the coyote story as a metaphor for the West. I come back to the coyote for the story of myself. Sometimes I am the one in the trap, unable to chew off my leg, unwilling to simply die. Somedays I place the bait. Both acts are mine. If coyote are anything, they are survivors. We are one, the elders sing.

I keep coming back to the coyote story to try to remember the moments after killing the coyote with exact clarity. I must get it right. Sometimes I see it as if I am watching myself from a distance. With the coyote's eyes. Through Katie. From behind the safety of binoculars, windshield, and scope. I couldn't shoot the coyote with my pistol because something in her eyes, amber like Katie's, reminded me of a familiar desperation that, from a distance, I couldn't see. Until I had to. The muzzle on the soft spot below the ear. The temple. So much like our own. I come back to the story because I still don't know who died that day in the Beartooth Front Country. I don't know if mine was an act of benevolence or mercy.

I've never returned to the place where I killed the coyote. It is lost on the prairie but perfectly mapped on the landscape of my memory. I sold the old blue Ford. Katie is dead and buried in the woods beyond my house. Two new dogs are in my life. A new man. The county vet, I am told, left town with someone else's wife. But that doesn't mean he doesn't haunt me. That I don't carry ghosts inside me.

But now the story is mine. And in this one, the coyote dies. There was no other way for this to end. Her leg is the leg broken in the trap pinned to the earth on a small rise in south-central Montana when a woman in a blue truck pulls up and the coyote, who knows nothing of mercy, is right to be afraid. The coyote, staring into the hazel eyes of her destroyer feels more pain before her final release. The coyote does not anthropomorphize, knows me only as predator, and sees only one human. The woman gets back in the truck, the lifeless body of a dog—for that is all she really is, isn't she? —lying on the seat beside her. She strokes coyote's fur as she drives, sings the songs her grandfather taught her, and where she finally buries the coyote is where the next story begins.

An Inheritance of Sound

Morning. Hells Canyon, Idaho, and I woke to birdsong. Like most mornings, at least in spring and summer, but this morning, it was crow and quail rather than robin and raven. A trio of crows had taken up stations in the limbs of a leaf-bare tree behind our camper. They began their chorus quite plaintively, and then, as a sermon might, the racket rose to a frenzied height, and they were gone with a flap of black wings. *They gave the coyote a funeral,* I whispered to my partner, Caleb, who lay beside me and didn't reply. We'd found the coyote the evening before, looking so alive, lying in the blackberry vines where he had been dumped. Blood song spilled from the hole in his chest when we lifted him. I rolled over on my stomach to look out of the window above our bed, just in time to see quail emerge from the dead branches and thorny blackberry vines that guarded the entrance to where Caleb had laid the coyote's body. One after another after another, they spilled from the brush, tender fists with feet, scratching, twitching, top notch bobbing as they explored the scene. Silenced turned to yawp and yips. *The ravens turned coyote into quail,* I whispered. In my mind, I saw the soft, tawny body breaking apart bird by bird until nothing remained but the quail and the bullet that killed the coyote.

It is through sound that I stay connected to my past…

The ring of the landline. The drop of a needle on a record and the forwarding of the film after the click of a shutter. It's through the sounds of sprinklers in the yard, the kind that tick tick tick and shudder their way in a circle. My father's reassuring voice on a cassette, my mother's laughter which is always sprinkled with words and head shakes, and *oh you kids*, never a roar like my sister's BRAAHAHA. The screen door opened and released to slap in its jam on an early summer afternoon when my dad came in, hot and smelling of alfalfa and gasoline from mowing the field behind the house. And there were songs we had sung as a family. Songs learned at Vacation Bible School. Songs my sister and I would never forget from cartoons we watched after coming home from school, where, in December, we would learn carols to sing in the annual Christmas Program held before we were released for the long break. Each grade taught the same song every year, so in kindergarten, while learning Rudolph, I looked forward to the fifth grade when we could sing about sheep safely grazing. I remember them all; I sing them, perk like a dog's ears to the sound of far-off thunder, or when I hear the song played at my husband's funeral. As sure as I know to answer *yes* when my mother calls my name, these sounds tell me who I am.

However, there is another choir of sounds that bespeak a different kind of knowing. Sounds that connect me to ancestors who also lived in the Rockies' shadow and to a larger community not defined by borders or ethnicity or familial name—songs that tell me where I am and, perhaps more importantly, where I come from. I learned the seasons by the arrival and leaving of birds such as meadowlark and the *cheerily cheerily cheer up* of robins. I knew the eerie whistling bugle of the bull elk meant autumn, the rising sound of a river that warned of floods, and the difference between the winds that meant rain and those that came as a shush from the setting sun. I learned thunder and hail on the roof and which way was north by the southbound honking geese. And all are embedded in a backdrop of silence provided by the rurality of my Rocky Mountain raising.

It is through sound that I stay connected to my ancestors...

I keep the window open at night. Sometimes only a crack, even in winter, at least while I sleep, not only for the air that smells as new as it does cold but for the sound that rides it into the darkened room. A decade ago, when I moved into the cabin near McCall, Idaho, the night sounds were thick and diverse, not unlike those of my rural growing in the Colorado Rockies. A dog barks at a deer, a cat screechs, and coyote sings. We are conditioned to fear the dark and that which we cannot see, even as some religions tell us to worship the unseen. But I neither worshipped nor feared the dark as a child, and even now, the dark elicits wonder. Night gave way to dreaming and dreaming to imagination. I created stories for coyotes, words for their songs—and I took the songs into me, with me to new places, and in my darkest hours, the ones not made black by night, I could howl and feel belonging in the song. It's a song known for thousands of years, sung by coyotes and heard by my ancestors and theirs. On a warm September morning, two people thousands of years apart could howl the same coyote song and speak the same language. A gift passed down through lives. An inheritance of sound.

It is through sound that I stay connected to place...

Nighttime in this more northern reach of the Rockies has offered new songs. When I first moved here ten years ago, I recall an evening when I woke my partner with an excited whisper of *what was that?* He wasn't asleep, also listening. *Fox,* he said. *Fox,* I thought, after the cry that sounded something like a cat, something like our dog's favorite squeaky toy, came through the screen again. I would learn nighthawk as well, then western tree frog, and one morning the grunt of a bear cub. After acclimating to their voices, I became unavoidably aware of the scraw of the Steller's Jay pair that lives near us year-round. The two, who we named White Above the Eye and Half Beak, had become equally used to us. When the feeder runs low, or we forget to rehang it in the morning, the pair will stand on the rail of our deck, face the sliding glass doors, and scraw until one of us appears with the mix of nuts and seed they devour. I became so tuned to their calls that one evening, just before dusk, I heard them and said to Caleb, "Something's wrong." It was a different cry, one I didn't know. Agitated. Fearful. I rose from my chair and searched the trees for them. The two, who seemed so large compared to every other bird that came to our feeder, now seemed small as they dove and flapped around a goose-sized Great Horned Owl perched in a lodgepole and looking into our glass panes. In this way, with careful listening, I have also developed a relationship with the land. This knowing goes beyond names, breeding seasons, and territories, and into the wisdom of relationship. The jays warned the other beings in our forest, alerting even us of danger. The owl, as magnificent as they are, is also often a harbinger of death. Indeed, for some that night, it was true.

It is quiet that most seek when they come to the mountains where I live. An escape from the busy sounds of the city, and they find it, at least to the degree for which they sought it. And perhaps because of this, and the beauty of the surrounding area, they want to stay. Or, at least they want to have a place to return on weekends or holidays. I think about the sounds that must have filled the nights on the glacial moraine I now call home. In the fall, there would have been the guttural whistle bugle of elk. Coyote song, particularly in the spring, in denning season, would have been in stereo, each calling from their places all over the forest. Then all may be silenced by the bigger dog, the wolf, whose howl sings in me deeper and brings me more wonder and excitement than any sound I know. And without the sound of cars and progress, what else might be heard? Sounds that perhaps we no longer have names for. Voices we can only wonder about.

This is how we can connect to the future, through the ancient echoes of the non-human beings that share this place...

The night before last, the moon was so bright it made plants grow. I pulled the window open wide, closed my eyes, and strained to hear the night beyond that of sleeping dogs, a humming refrigerator, and the soft in and out breaths of my partner. It has been a year since I've heard a fox. Gone, too, is the soughing of pine, a sighing sound of wind through trees that used to lull me to sleep on nights when the weather was moving. There is still the rumble of distant thunder. In winter, the thud of snow that the pines surrounding us drop to our metal roof. The gentle tap of rain and the occasional night hawk. But the song I miss most is the song of the coyote. I haven't heard their music in at least two years. Trees are felled as the housing developments grow. Coyotes are found shot and tossed aside. The sounds now: surround-sound TV, a neighbor yelling for their dog to be quiet, another recent neighbor to our area yelling at someone unknown to fuck off. Another car whirrs down the road. A semi pulls the Jake brake.

A few miles from Hells Canyon Dam, in a cave above the Snake River, a petroglyph is painted in red ochre, the image of a salmon. I can only wonder at the number of years it has been there, one thousand or ten thousand. Still, in the twilight part of the cave, just before it turns to dark, the salmon is forever captured, moving upstream. It is the only salmon left above Hells Canyon Dam, which, when completed in 1966, ended a migration thousands of years old. In the town of Stanley, residents said that the river that once woke them with the sound of running salmon had gone quiet. In the hearts of the people who have been here for over 16,000 years, a new silence entered. Loss of that kind makes a sound that can only be felt, that takes your breath and leaves no song.

I'm not sure how to immortalize the coyote song for those who will live here after me. Words can only do so much, and humans aren't equipped with the coyote's ability to sing, nor do we understand their language. Coyotes once seemed so familiar that it was almost foolish to doubt that they never would be. They were abundant. So, I assume, many thought of the salmon. And the wolf. Thought, too, of the enduring voices of their parents and children.

Hells Canyon Revival

"And always, in this search, a person might find that she is already there, at the center of the world. It may be a broken world, but it is glorious nonetheless." —Linda Hogan

"Our task is to enter the dream of Nature and interpret the symbols." —E.L. Grant Watson

This canyon does not abide a trail.

The steepness of its walls, and the scree that covers them, suggests a downward movement. But we are going up. Up toward the base of massive limestone cliffs.

The dogs have an easier time of it. My partner Caleb and I scramble and slide, reaching for sage and ninebark as handholds. What trails exist are likely made by deer and elk coming down from their ridgetop refuges to drink from Allison Creek. I make my way to a flat section and catch my breath. From here, it is a matter of guesswork. The way to Redfish Cave is not marked. It is not on a map. The entrance cannot be seen from below. Rumor and vague directions are our guides. Two false starts lead us nowhere; on the third, we walk a narrow precipice, squeeze through mountain mahogany, and find ourselves at the entrance.

I wrap my fingers around the steel bars that are cemented into the mouth of the cave and press my face into the darkness, eyes searching as if for a prisoner who might walk into view. The day is cool and rainy, the metal cold against my face. When my eyes finally adjust, I see it. At the far end of the entrance to Redfish Cave, in an area called the twilight zone, an ochre pictograph of a salmon.

The air escaping the cave smells like the earth when rain first touches it. Petrichor. My eyes become adjusted to the darkness, and I see the fine soil, cave dust, and the loose rocks and leaves that cover the floor. I am eager to go in. Desperate to sit in the place where the artist sat. To look closely at the dots, each no bigger than a fingerprint, in the form of a salmon. I want to touch those fingerprints, made of blood and plant as if I could touch the past, as if I can somehow connect to a history I carry in my blood. An ache to connect with this Plateau artist moves my fingers toward the art. I reach out to the salmon, my arm a bridge over which only my understanding passes, stopping short of the colored and cold cavern wall.

We carefully make our way down from Redfish Cave, down Allison Creek, and finally to the Snake River, to the murky, dam-stilled waters. When we reach the reservoir, the salmon takes over my thoughts. The pictograph is about a quarter mile above the channel where the Snake River once flowed free. For hundreds, probably thousands of years, this canyon was home to Nez Perce. Now it is a National Recreation Area and designated Wilderness. The recent titles provide protection for the area and places like Redfish Cave but came after the river's damming and the subsequent burial of similar sites, other art. Nearly all traces of indigenous occupation are buried under 200 feet of water and layers of silt and debris. Salmon have not swum these waters since 1967.

From 1956 through 1967, three dams were built in succession along this part of the Snake: Brownlee, Oxbow, and Hells Canyon. Idaho Power, the company commissioned to build them, agreed to create and maintain a viable way in which salmon and steelhead would be able to by-pass the dams and continue their natural migration to their natal waters, some as far as 300 miles upstream.

In the fall of 1958, near the completion of the Oxbow Dams, the attempt to trap and transport the salmon fifteen miles upriver past Brownlee Dam, failed. Four thousand fish died in splash pools below the dam and seven thousand more in transport. Eleven thousand salmon. Two and a half times the human population of the town I live in.

The disaster, dubbed the Oxbow Incident, resulted in a federal investigation, but no successful remedy could be found, outside a promise by Idaho Power for a handful of hatcheries. At Hells Canyon Dam, no attempt at all was made for fish passage. In 1967, when the entire three-dam project was completed, thousands of years of salmon migration ended. The Snake River had seen its last run. The only salmon remaining above Hells Canyon Dam is painted in Redfish Cave.

Caleb and I return to Hells Canyon every spring. Escaping the deep snow at our cabin in McCall, we embrace spring at this lower elevation. Trailing our camper behind the truck, we exchange our dichromatic backdrop of pine green and white for one painted with yellow arrowleaf, pink cherry blossoms, and bluebird song. Our camp is alive with sound and color. Parked next to the reservoir that serves as the border between Idaho and Oregon, we slip our canoe into the Snake and paddle across the water, then hike up Spring Creek, where we eventually gain a ridgetop.

From our perch on the canyon wall, we barely make out the green dot that is our canoe. Around and above us, an endless panorama of buckskin and blue. Across the river, we can see the 9000-foot peaks of the Seven Devils, and behind us are the two million acres of the Wallowa-Whitman National Forest. Our feet rest on a ledge, soles facing the deepest gorge in the United States and 36 miles of a reservoir. We eat lunch among wolf tracks and elk droppings. I pull out my notebook and try to capture, in a few words, the vastness of it all. But, like the camera lens, it is impossible to frame it. I cross out what I have written and pocket the notebook. Cumulus clouds pile in from the south, and the air darkens and tosses the dogs' ears. We hike back down to the canoe moments ahead of the rain.

That evening, I lie in bed and stare out across the water to a knob of land we have named Bone Island. It's not fair to call it an island as it is part of the bar that the dams have stranded. It is also unfair to give it such an ominous name, but there is a lot of unfair naming in this region. The name Hells Canyon, for example, is undoubtedly not apropos for an area that holds so much beauty, so much life. The Seven Devils that guard the canyon may seem wicked to those who attempt their summits, but the name belies their Teton-like grandeur. Who chose these names and why? How do we begin to explain the complexity and exquisiteness of such a landscape with just a name? What did first people of this landscape call the bony prominences that hold the last light of evening? What words explained this canyon to them? I think of how I might rename it and falter, tripped by my need to tell everything I know about the canyon in a couple of words. Frustrated with the task, I roll over and go to sleep.

We wake to rain falling on the metal roof, so I decide to stay in the camper and write. Outside, geese honk and make their loud landings onto the murky water. Swans float by. Ducks call from the shore of the island. Inside, I make little progress.

Like before, on the ridge, I discard lines as soon as they are written. I have a poem in mind, a piece that I can see and sense, but I cannot bring it to paper. The words feel forced, planned. Rather than giving the image control, in this case, the river's image, I try to control it. Force it into my own idea, tossing in erudition and clever enjambment so that before it is fully born, I have pushed it back into the dark. The aluminum roof thrums with the rain. I put away my writing reach for a poetry anthology, and thumb the pages for inspiration. Instead, I find myself analyzing techniques.

I pace the short length of the camper, reading aloud. Midway through a Wallace Stevens poem, I close the book and trade it for a thick volume of theory. I hope that by understanding the construction, methods, and terminology used to make poetry, I will find the instruction I need to complete the poem. I am searching for a formula, a blueprint. I look at the lines I have written; they're solid, intelligent, and fit the definition of a poem, but they are flat on the page. The piece lacks heart, lacks wildness, is given over to too much management. Outside, the rain trembles the dammed waters, gentle thunder echoes through the canyon. I put the poems and books away and pull on my raincoat. We will drive to the end of the road. We will go to the dam itself.

Parked beneath the dam, the windshield wipers work to clear our view while we stare at the massive cement wall that holds back the Snake River. A single outlet is open, spewing water 150 feet before it crashes into the pool beneath. From here, the dam appears as both a castle and a prison. Wires running from the parapet could as easily be gossamer as razor, yet they are neither, merely cables carrying as much as 391 megawatts of electricity. I cannot comprehend how much power that is or how the river was managed to create it. But I can see the art in the craftsmanship of the dam—the almost impossibility of it. And I am aware this art, this feat of engineering, was championed as a source of renewable energy. It is genius, and it is deadly, and I am unable to forget the cost of this structure: the thousands of salmon that died, the drowned cultural history, the river's freedom. It is true that I have become dependent on electricity, on this structure, but true also that I depend on wildness to power my imagination. As the sun breaks from the clouds, rainbows rise from the mist of cascading water. This very place is both the end of the line for spawning salmon and the source of energy that lights our home. Across the river, a mountain goat ascends the steep canyon wall. A snow-white kid follows at her hooves. Idaho has the cheapest power in the United States.

Nez Perce, unlike many other tribes, did not rely on specific drawings for communication. When they painted, it was spontaneous, unplanned, and often unexplained to even the closest family members. The meaning of the art in the cave would always be left open to the interpreter to guess at, dream about, and wonder at. Since learning this, I have given up trying to find meaning for what I see on the smooth wall of Redfish Cave, and instead, I let the art move my emotions. I allow art the art to be as the artist felt when making it. In doing so, I am allowed an intimacy with the artist that is uninhibited by contemporary knowledge. This I find the most inspiring. The most like nature itself.

Archibald Ritchie and Dave Eckles, early settlers to the Hells Canyon area, planted an orchard and extensive gardens on Big Bar, where we are camped and where the two are now buried. The Eckles Ranch, as it was called, provided most of the fruit and vegetables to the mining camps in the Seven Devils and the surrounding area. Their trees still line the terraces that serve as the campground. The trees that have survived now provide refreshment in the summer when temperatures in the canyon rise well above 90 degrees. A sign, placed by the Forest Service, explains the men's history and the ranch in detail. No mention is made of the people who lived here before Ritchie and Eckles. To learn the Native history of Big Bar, one must do her own research.

Pre-dam photographs show Big Bar as a grassy, meadow-like slope, where archaeologists found tools and hunting implements suggesting hundreds of years of Indian encampment. From places like Big Bar and throughout the drainage, it is presumed that Native people fished for salmon and hunted deer, elk, and mountain goats. Walking Big Bar, Caleb and I have admired the hollows of pit houses, but most art, shelters, and other leavings were destroyed, collected, or now lie under the turbid water. The archaeologists' reports, black and white photos, and the artifacts they found are locked away in a steel cabinet in urban offices throughout Idaho and Oregon. I can't help seeing the irony in this as well. Why not just leave the items where they lie and let the water cover them? Why does the government presume the right to possess the arrowheads and tattered parfleches? Shouldn't they belong to the descendants of this region? I know I am not the first to ask this.

That evening, Caleb and I sit beside a campfire and ponder a pre-dam Hells Canyon. On a warm night such as this, would the canyon walls echo the sound of song and laughter of Nimiipuu celebrating the coming spring? Would we, unable to translate, still hear their stories as they were passed along the shores? No, we realize. Though their fires might light the walls, little would be heard over the constant roar of the river. Quiet and darkness, smoke and firelight frame us. I stare toward the water and try to imagine the sound and force of the undammed river. I cannot. I wonder about the day the river was dammed and the animals that must have fled from its rising. I see deer and rabbits, snakes, and crickets rushing to drainages, ascending the steep terrain as the water follows them. I imagine the silence that fills the canyon as the same as the silence that fills the mind when I place empty palms to my ears.

We wake early to clear skies and a light breeze that carries pure white apple blossoms around our camp. We decide to make the longest of the mapped hikes in the region. A loop that will take us through three significant drainages, over five ridges, and finally funnel us out with Eckles Creek a mile or so from where we are camped. Point-to-point, the hike is about 15 miles. We begin the first two miles from the camper, beside the reservoir, on the road. The sun is not quite over the eastern ridge.

A mile into the walk, we hear the honk of a goose. But it is somehow different from those companionable honks we have heard all week. It seems urgent. Agitated. We see the goose above us, its slender body cutting the brightening blue. It is alone and then it is not. Something is catching up to it. Often, I see raptors being chased by smaller birds protecting their nests, but this is not that. It is a predator behind the goose, a bird almost as big as the goose itself. Its white chest and head give it away—a bald eagle. I pull in my breath, *no*, and put my hand on Caleb's arm. *Come on, goose, come on.* One wingbeat and the eagle is a length away from the goose. Two more and the eagle grabs for the goose, but the goose dives and, for a moment, escapes. In seconds the eagle overcomes it, and the sky and canyon quiet.

We watch the eagle carry the limp body to the other side of the reservoir, where it lands on a boulder. I let go of the breath I'd been holding. I wanted the goose to escape the eagle, to see the non-predator prevail, but this is nature. And nature's rules of survival are exactly as they should be without human interference. In the moments that follow, neither of us speaks. Caleb and I stand at the guardrail and look toward the rock where the eagle has landed. After a few moments, we turn away and continue toward the trailhead.

As we hike the switchbacks to the ridge above Kinney Creek, I jot down questions in my notebook. Why had I wanted the goose to escape? To spare me the pain of death? Because it is my nature to want the underdog to prevail? What is it in me that craves this wildness but also fears it? To allow it to be without my interference, without my expectation? What if it was the eagle and not the goose that had been under attack? When I let the questions go, I begin writing lines to a new poem. I cross nothing out. By the time we reach the summit above Kinney Creek, I have filled four pages.

I sit with my back against a pine, and my eyes drift down to the reservoir. Before the dams, the water rose and fell with snowmelt and rain. Thousands of salmon spawned up the Snake to rivers and streams far beyond. After spawning, their deaths would have provided food for grizzlies, birds, insects, and eventually the trees and shrubs that grow in the riparian space along the river's edge. The dams not only ended migrations but also led to the loss of other beings upstream. Fishermen, both Native and white, could no longer count on salmon for food. In Stanley, Idaho, a couple of hundred miles upstream, the residents reported that the river had grown silent, lifeless, as if the river's spirit, Salmon, were taken in exchange for electricity. I look across the reservoir to the ridgeline through air breathed by elk and wolves. Something inside of me aches. Is longing for the past I cannot have, or hungry for a future I cannot imagine? It feels like the place between regret and promise.

Here, in the wildness of Hells Canyon, also lies the result of man's vast and brilliant imagination. Behind me, a mostly unaltered wilderness with some of the most rugged terrain in the Pacific Northwest. Below me, a display of human ingenuity that buried millions of years of natural history and thousands of years of cultural history. The Snake River's power is transmuted into electricity that brings light to back porches and refrigerates milk as far away as Montana. I try to block one out, as if covering one eye with my hand so that I might see the other more clearly, but I know that it takes both eyes to understand this view. I want to love the wilderness while admiring the beautiful architecture of the dam. Embrace the Native history without condemning the colonial present. Can I forgive the bald eagle, even as it steals the goose from the sky? I want to, but I don't know where to begin.

Here in Hells Canyon, where humans and wildness connect and collide, where history and future are held in the same water, where loss and potential are as opposing and eroding as water carving rock, I am trying to learn how to accept and how to change. I am attempting to answer the question that is being asked by many in this region: How do we continue to live in the West, to enjoy the lifestyle and the cheap electricity and the roads and the advances we seem to have made while preserving the past, the open spaces, the spirit of the river, and the solitude we crave? I have looked for the answer in books, I searched for it in the dam's blueprints, I read for it on the historical sign, but it is not written. The answer is greater than the sum of its questions. I think that it lies in the return of the salmon to the river as much as it lives in the salmon painted on the wall of Redfish Cave.

It is our last morning in the canyon. We rise early, moving slowly, as we make breakfast and pack lunch. Even the dogs resist the inevitable leaving of a place that has, in just a few days, come to feel like home. None of us bounds out of the camper. When we put the canoe in the water, we do it so gently that the ducks swimming nearby do not startle as we float silently by. The morning light is brilliant. We watch deer as they feed across a sunlit slope and do not let the grumble of ravens hasten our movement. From somewhere behind us, we hear quail call *chi-ka-go* and a canyon wren frames the scene with a loud cascade of song. We drift toward the boulder the eagle had landed on and beach the canoe.

I don't know what I was expecting: A bright orange foot? A beak? Carnage the likes of roadkill? But what awaited us was none of that. There, amidst the black lichen, on granite surrounded by encroaching blackberry vines, was a drift of snow-white goose down. A thin breeze lifted, then settled the feathers with a sigh. I lift two from the pile and place them in my breast pocket.

We paddle back in silence. I do not look to the canyon walls or blue sky, but down instead at the smooth surface of water, so calm it is as if we are floating in a mirror. The blue of sky, green of sage and pine, and the gray of limestone are repeated on the water's surface. Carp, the most abundant fish in the reservoir, lounge close to the surface, warming in the morning sun. We float within inches before they break the stillness and dive into darkness. I try to follow one of their shapes into the depths. I marvel at the adaptability of the carp and mourn the absence of the salmon. Somewhere beneath me lives history covered with silt. I want the canoe to float us back in time so that just once, I might hear the roar of the Snake River in spring, and see its wildness crash from boulder to boulder. I want to hear singing, watch the artist climb the slope to the cave. I want to bring back the salmon to revive the spirit of the river. I reach to the water and when I touch it, I startle my own reflection.

If you go past the gate guarding Redfish Cave, past the ochre salmon forever swimming upstream, you will come to two panels of art that cannot be seen from the entrance. Stop for a moment and wonder at what you see. Is it a pregnant woman? A man who swallowed the sun? Is the being beside it a mountain goat? A dog? Do not mind the shiny black millipede crawling on the damp ceiling above you, and do not touch the art as modern fingers erase ancient design. To your right is a tunnel your body will barely squeeze through. Get on your belly. Let the spiders walk across your bridge of fingers. Pull yourself through the passage and into the dark womb of the cave. You will need light to see the ten-thousand-year-old formations, but you cannot touch them either; they appear strong but are fragile, like so many of the seemingly formidable structures in this canyon. Now douse the light. Become friendly with the darkness, the unknown. And before you leave, before you return to the bright world that awaits, remember the packrat that lives here. She's watching you. In her amber midden is a single downy goose feather, is the story of Hells Canyon.

Aspen

The sun is still on the edge of the horizon even though it is past eight o'clock. The canted light makes the aspen on the side of the road seem more animated than usual. Spotted black and white like palomino hides, they quiver with the same anticipation as wild horses. I am standing in the middle of Boydstun Street in McCall, Idaho. Caleb, my partner of six years, is kneeling before me. We are dressed up. We have just left a wedding.

It is unseasonably warm, and it has been all year. I can feel the rocky surface of the asphalt beneath the thin leather soles of my old boots. It warms my feet, which have become still and heavy. I wonder if I should call the police. I do not have a gun; my fingers worry the handle of the knife that lay in my pocket.

"I thought it was a dog," the driver says as he runs his fingers through his salt-and-pepper gray hair. I do not look at him because I am angry at him, because I fear what I might say. I look instead at the fawn that lies at my feet. "I hardly felt it," he concludes. There are just the four of us: the driver, Caleb, me, and the fawn. The road is quiet. We are standing on the faded centerline. The fawn's eyes are huge, black, and glossy, blinking rapidly. Pain and fear hold her rigid. She bleats softly toward the aspen, but there is no reply. She is panting, she will not live; she cannot survive. This knowledge is a pain I feel in my chest, and I know it as regret. I bend to stroke the soft fur of her small, pricked ears.

Caleb slides his arms beneath the fawn's body. She looks like a toddler being carried to bed. She turns her head, glancing again toward the aspen. She does not struggle. He carries her to the graveled side of the road, away from further harm by cars. The sun has fallen behind the mountains; the light is that of our headlights which hold the scene as if it were being acted out on a stage. Still, no one drives by. We will not leave the fawn to die alone, nor do we expect her to live. It is a decision made before she was hit, part of an unspoken code. In my pocket, I feel the cold steel of the knife. It knows its dark purpose like an old soldier knows their duty. In the cold strength of the steel, I remember the blood of the doe it was used to kill eleven years earlier.

There is a moment of thunderous silence when metal meets flesh. Anyone who has ever been in or witnessed an accident will tell you that it happens as if projected on a mute screen, each frame in slow motion. First, the arc of the dark blue side mirror as it descends onto and bounces along the pavement. Then, the shower of glass refracting late daylight, heavy rain of headlamp, and amber turn signal lens showers onto asphalt, each shard as unique as a snowflake. The metal hood wrinkles like a brow furrowing, and blue paint peels from the body to expose the dull metal beneath.

Over a decade before, on a road far from this one, my husband Randy and I witnessed this accident through the windshield of our pickup. The doe is performing a grotesque ballet; the car throws her into a petite jeté, but she fails the landing and falls with legs splayed on the macadam, the yellow line perfectly dividing her broken and unbroken halves. Sound returns then, a country ballad wafts through the truck speakers. Words come to my lips, but I do not speak them. I wait to hear the scream of the minivan's tires against the cool October pavement, but it does not come. The vehicle does not stop.

We saw this coming. I like to think that Randy had blinked the truck's headlights at the car, a rural warning of deer or patrolmen, but I never asked him. The doe was standing in the aspen, feeding on the grass beneath; several of her herd had already safely crossed. Why she had waited for the moment when the blue car passed to join them, I do not know. Seven does now run across the field toward the Beartooth Mountains; one lies bleating in the evening light. Her hooves scratch at the rocky pavement. Her front end is trying to pull up her back, trying to pull herself off the road, sensing danger too late.

It is 2005, eleven years before Caleb and I kneel at the side of Boydstun Street in the bright lights of our idling car and stroke the new and tawny fur of a week's old and broken fawn in McCall, Idaho. I am in Montana, between the towns of Roberts and Red Lodge. On a stretch of road known as Deer Alley; Highway 212, notorious for its scenic beauty, is cursed by those who have replaced quarter panels, headlamps, or entire vehicles after run-ins with wildlife.

Randy and I are dressed up. We are on our way to dinner in Red Lodge. We are meeting friends. This is an unexpected stop, and it angers both of us. Not because we would be late but because the driver of the minivan did not stop. Because the doe is still alive, still scraping the asphalt with her hooves. Randy is pounding the black steering wheel with the square palms of his ranch-calloused hands. "God dammit," he repeats over and over, "God fucking dammit."

We are not innocent of these collisions. Only months before, just as we crossed the bridge over Rock Creek on our way to an early morning appointment at the veterinarian's office in Billings, a grown whitetail jumped in front of the same truck we now sit in. Randy could not stop. Could not swerve for the bridge's edges. By the time I shouted *deer!* the buck had begun its roll over our truck, its antlers breaking against the windshield, body crushing the hood as Randy and I ducked in fear of the buck coming through the glass.

Randy drove the truck to the shoulder, radiator steaming, but it would go no further. We got out of the truck unharmed and walked into the borrow pit to find the deer. I do not think either of us assumed the buck would be alive, and he was not. His torso held, but other parts of the buck were strewn about the ditch and road. Blood muddied the dirt. We stood together, beside the broken life, neither of us knowing that the brokenness before us would soon be a tragedy we would share. We called our neighbors and a tow truck. Two weeks later, the truck came back from the shop with an enormous black bumper made of two-inch steel bolted to the front. Randy would never hit another deer.

Back on 212 some months later, Randy cuts the engine but leaves the headlights on. I get out, walk around the front of the truck, past the new bumper, and join him next to the deer. She was alert, in shock, eyes all pupil, mouth open, and panting. Her legs had relaxed, but her eyes were fixed on the other does which were now only dots in a field. She tried to rise, but every time her charcoal hooves got the slightest purchase on the macadam, she would fall splay-legged to the ground. I think of how this reminds me of a scene from Bambi, the one of him and Flower on the ice, and I am ashamed.

Randy grabs her left front leg, and I take her right. She does not fight as we pull her body to the side of the road. She is heavy, and her muscles tense. Randy and I are hunters and have killed and dragged our share of deer, but never a living one. We are moving now with the actions that were written out on a script of our rural raising. There is an animal before us whose life we could not save, so it is our role, out of duty or benevolence, to end the animal's suffering.

In the console of my truck is a .40 caliber handgun. It is there, not for protection, but for times like this. I grew up a ranch kid; I grew up rural. I knew of the damage vehicles, barbed wire, and gopher holes did to animals. I knew when it was too late to call a vet. I learned how fast a pulled trigger could end pain. But the truck is at home, the gun safe in the console. We need something else. In Randy's truck is the knife my father had given me. The blade was only five inches but was sharp.

I hand it to Randy, who pulls the silver edge open. "It'll have to do," he says and strokes the head of the doe.

When field dressing, or gutting, a deer, the esophagus is cut by reaching both hands in the chest cavity, up the throat and neck, grasping the incredibly strong cartilage, and sawing it free from the back of the mouth. In this manner, the rest of the intestines will follow, spilling out below or beside the animal into blood and hair and dirt and often snow. The knife my father gave me was for this purpose, as well as castrating calves and gutting fish. I kept it sharp for its work not understanding, until years later, that it was not the knife I wanted but the feeling of responsibility that came with it. I did not understand, until that evening on the side of the road, why my father waited so long to give me the knife. Though I was a year past thirty, I did not understand that the gift was double-edged: with the knife came trust, and with trust came choices and sometimes pain that could not be avoided.

The knife blade captures and releases the last of the daylight. Randy bends before the deer. He asks me to hold her legs, to keep her head back. The breeze that comes at day's end moves through the golden aspen leavens. My hands shake.

Brown and white ticks run from the doe's fur and up our arms. I do not move to brush them away as I had before. Randy is parting the thick white hair on the side of the doe's neck. He is looking for the carotid artery; cutting the esophagus is not enough. He needs to stop the blood to the brain; to stop the heart. He exposes the doe's skin and inserts the tip swiftly, expertly. Blood tears from the wound. His hand operates independently now from his grief and anger. He is a medevac pilot. He served in the Army. He has seen blood before. He has known accidents.

Randy and I met two years earlier, almost to the date. It was autumn. Red Lodge. A blind date. When he walked into the bar, I spilled my purse. I couldn't speak when he said hello. He was tall and humble, in pressed Wranglers and a silver Stetson. He had a kind face and a cleft chin. He looked like Buzz Lightyear, and months later, on

Valentine's Day, he presented me with a picture of himself dressed up as the Disney astronaut and signed, in black marker, *You and Me, To Infinity and Beyond! Love, Randy.* We were married in a private ceremony. Only two years later, by the side of the Clarks Fork River near Cody, Wyoming, in the fading light of a June day, I would lie alone next to his body, the taste of his vomit and river water on my lips. A widow at the age of 32.

I have my knee on the doe's legs. She is still trying to stand, but I hold her head to the earth. It is a position like the one my body had become used to branding calves. The bleat of pain that came from the hot iron hitting their hides was different than the one working to escape her sleek throat. The calves felt anguish but would live. I was doing work, ranch work, and I had learned that the discomfort of the calves was the lifeblood of the ranch. I never cried, not even when a cow died. The sound coming from the deer begins to feel like a wailing. I try to steel myself, to understand this too as work, but her struggle to live, her wail into the darkness awakens in me a grief I did not know I harbored. Hot tears run down my cheeks, followed by sobs. I hear myself say, *please.* I wanted it to be over. *Why won't she die? Why is this taking so long? Please. Please.*

Randy does not look away from the doe when he tells me to go back to the truck. I let go of her legs and failure walks with me as I leave. Failure to help. Failure to stay with the doe through her pain. And a greater sense that I failed the purpose of the knife, the trust of my father. I sit in the silent cab, unable to see Randy or the deer. Crying. Pitying myself. Feeling small in the big country and helpless under the dark sky that is falling around us.

Randy rises and brushes the knees of his jeans. I watch him pull the lifeless body to the side of the road, and my eyes trace the dark line of blood that follows them both into the ditch and then into the waiting aspen. He steps back onto the highway, then bends to wipe the blade of my knife in the cheat grass and returns the edge to its handle. There is blood on his good jeans now. Blood on his hands. His head and body bent forward as if he had just finished two days' hard work. I watch one headlight hold him, then the other. He enters the cab and we sit for a moment in silence. "I'll put a new edge on it," he says, handing me the knife. "I think I hit bone." He turns the truck around in the middle of the highway and we drive home.

Months later, by the Clarks Fork, I will recall that October evening and again feel the shame of leaving Randy to the chore of death. I had left the river's edge to go for beer and snacks and had left him with a friend to paddle their kayaks to the take-out. I would meet them there, meet them at the end of the run. We would be full of life. We would return to camp and he would tell me about the day and we would go to bed together and when we woke, everything would be as it was, our lives in the palm of my hand. But it wasn't. I lay like the deer hit on the side of the road. Shattered and at once alive. But unlike the deer, Randy died alone, with no witness to what happened or how. I could not get past the feeling that again I had let him down. I tried to wrap my arms around him, ignoring the strangeness of not feeling his arms come around me. When at last I couldn't move him, I pressed my face to his wet suit and spoke impossible prayers. My hand, pressed against his chest, searching for his familiar heartbeat. Already I was replaying the last moments. Him across the river, waving. Him, smiling. Him, signaling with his hand to throat that they were done, no more rapids. Him, pressing his lips to his palm and blowing a kiss across the river that would kill him.

I hold the knife with the same determination that I held Randy's hand on that October night when he killed the doe. "I can feel her heart," Caleb says, and I am back on the summer road in McCall. His large hand covers the doe's speckled chest. It is almost dark. The air is still and growing cold. I raise my skirt and kneel in the gravel, feeling grateful for the pain when it comes. Caleb and I are side-by-side, the fawn in front of us, the pepper-haired man is still watching. When he sees me unsheathe the knife, he returns to his car and leaves.

If you live long enough, and if you pay attention, you will recognize that patterns form in your life. Some bear repeating, but others can so drastically destroy you that all effort must be taken to change them. The days and years that followed Randy's death found me in every state of grief and destruction. The pieces of me that his drowning left along the Clarks Fork I had collected only to break again along the shores of the next decade of my life. Then I met Caleb. And slowly, I began to rebuild myself, to piece back together a life, a future. To live again. In time I understood that the knife was only a tool; it was the hand that held the knife that mattered. And though Caleb's hand was open, waiting for me to hand him the knife, I had no intention of doing so. It would be my hand that guided the blade. As I leaned into my work, I felt the sting of tears and the bitter taste of regret. I would not leave either alone. I would not turn away from the pain of death. I would not let the past repeat. The blood would be on my hands and fate could do with me as it pleased. And this sounds selfless, it sounds like I was trying to save Caleb, but the truth is, it was my own misery I feared. I would kill the fawn to save myself.

With the headlights' glare nearly blinding me, I steel myself as I do before I pull the trigger on my rifle. Suddenly, killing the fawn is something I am merely watching my hands do. I turn the blade's sharp edge to an angle, and in a movement that looks like I am stroking the deer's neck, I bring the blade to the fawn's skin. I do not cry.

"She's gone," Caleb whispers before the first drop of blood rises to the knife. "Her heart stopped." I do not ask if he is sure. Her eyes have gone matte. Her head angled now in a death repose I have seen so many times in her kind: tipped back, mouth open, breathing spirit to sky. I twist the blade back into its handle and release it in my pocket. Once more, Caleb rolls the fawn into his arms, her head hanging limply at his side, and walks her into the dark and waiting aspen.

I have been told, and have come to believe, that life happens in the margins. On the sides of roads and rivers, just out of the firelight, just off the trail. I have learned that life encompasses, just as wholly, death, and thus they are sistered in this liminal place, a place of constant change, of true aliveness. I spend much of my time in this space between places. My own life somewhat stable, but I'm keenly aware of the lives and deaths that live with me. I have learned, too that the health and wellbeing of everything from forests to relationships can be determined by the edges surrounding them. A tree browns on the leaves to show a dying root, the outskirts of town reflect the vitality of the city, the lines in the hand tell of a person's life, and the side of the road holds all that we discard, all that we may collide with, as we move from place to place. From this liminal holding, I have learned to witness.

At home, Caleb starts a fire in the woodstove, then stands and stares out our tall windows into the dark forest surrounding our cabin. As the heat and light grow behind him, the windows become mirrors, and I stare at his reflection, as he stares at his hand.

"I have never felt something die before," he says without looking up, then comes to the couch and sits beside me. He lays his open hand atop mine. "Her last heartbeat is still in my palm." The fire has grown bright enough that I can see the deep lines. The roads and rivers across his broad hand. We fall into reverence staring into his palm. Staring as if we might see something there, as if what we hoped to see could be seen at all.

Lake 8

The map I am given is worn. The crease where it has been unfolded and refolded is delicate. The lakes and tributaries are hand-drawn, their labels in neat, elegant cursive. The paper has become soft, like the inside of a doe's ear; velvety. The images and words have been photocopied so many times that they are starting to fade; the shorelines of the unnamed lakes are missing, the water flowing from their outlets never reaches the main channel. If the map were not labeled Stillwater Lakes, I would think this a drawing of ovaries and fallopian tubes, and as I look from the map to the miles of mountains, lakes, and valleys before me, I am reminded of how like the geography of a woman's generative anatomy this landscape is.

I am trying to get oriented. To line up the map, which lacks a compass rose, with the horseshoe-shaped lake below us. My partner, Caleb, and our two dogs, Carhartt and Cisco, are with me. We have just hiked to the top of Cache Mountain; it is the first of three days we will spend exploring an unnamed chain of lakes in the Frank Church Wilderness. I turn the map ninety degrees until the crescent-shaped lake on paper lines up with the one in the trees below us. According to the map, this is Lake 5. Caleb glasses the area around the lake and says there is a good tent site, a dry mud flat near the water. We will put our tent there and sleep on the flattest ground that we've slept on all summer. This will be home for the next three days.

Though a faint trail, made of a decommissioned road to a mine, then reestablished as a fire line, could be found to the top of Cache

Mountain, no trail will lead us to the lake. We will have to make our own way for the mile or so down the steep slope to the sapphire green that lies below us. Caleb goes first, the dogs behind him, and I fall in last, always slower than the others as I stop to take photos, taste pine needles, or rub sage, when I can find it, between my palms and then hold them, like a breathing mask over my nose and mouth, inhaling the sweet and sometimes spicy clean smell of it. More often than not, I am stooped over looking at rocks or tracks or the slow progress of a snail and totally lose sight of or run directly into Caleb.

Such is the case this morning as I am nearly on his heels while he is stopped in front of me. Black binoculars to his blue eyes, he is looking down at the valley beneath us and at the soft gentle slope that slowly drains the water from Lake 5. He turns to me. Whispers, *Goats.* I smile. I know what it means to him to see mountain goats in this part of the Wilderness. What it means to the Wilderness ecosystem to have them here. For years, overhunting and the accumulating presence of people have driven down their populations. The remaining goats left for more remote parts of the Wilderness. That they are here now is a sign that the land is coming back to what biologists like Caleb believe is a natural state. *Eight,* he says, *maybe ten.* He hands me the binoculars and I look. As perfect as clouds against sky, they stand white against green. Slow and lazy, too. But they are wary of predators; as soon as they hear or smell us, they will dissolve like the clouds they resemble, drifting up, dissipating into the rocks and crags that are their natural terrain.

It is August in West Central Idaho. Most of the wildflowers are gone from the ridgelines and hillsides. The beargrass has bloomed, the long stalks have fallen. The arrowleaf is a memory held for spring; only a few scarlet paintbrush bloom alongside a yellow daisy, ubiquitous, but whose name always eludes me. This isn't typical. It is dryer than normal. We have not had a storm since early June, and the lack of rain can be felt and heard and is carried in the air around us. The grass crunches as we step, the brush of leaves against our bare legs, once tender and welcome, is sharp and stings. There is the sound of airplanes carrying people or water or supplies to a nearby fire whose smoke burns our eyes and curtains a view that would otherwise have been so vast that we would lose our sense of size in it, which would drown us with awe.

We move downhill quickly. Gravity and terrain allow us big steps, and soon we have dropped almost a thousand feet. As we near the lake, it is as if we are stepping back in seasons. Brown grass has turned back to green. The smoke above us, an amorphous ceiling. We breath easily now. Mountain Gentian lays a carpet of the most exquisite blue before us, and we find ourselves stepping carefully among the low plants, not wanting to crush a single blossom, not wanting to carry the scent of that crime on our soles. We shed our packs on the mudflat and walk together to the water's edge.

The map was the result of an alpine lake survey taken in 1996. Though the drawing may have been made years before, the writing belongs to Peggy, a colleague of Caleb's at the US Forest Service office in McCall, Idaho. Caleb found and copied this version, then handed it to me when we reached Cache Peak. When I ask, Caleb tells me that among many other tasks that Peggy completed as a seasonal employee since the 70s, such as riparian surveys and road inventories, she also performed lake surveys. Packing an inflatable raft, gill nets, fishing poles, her tent, and camping supplies, she hiked from lake to lake to determine whether fish had survived from decades earlier stocking efforts by Idaho Fish and Game. I admire and envy her work. I envy her strength. That she came to the Wilderness by herself. Alone. I think about her long days of silence and hiking, and the map becomes more than a map of a place, but of a woman's way in the wild. I am glad it is a woman's work. That it holds within its careful drawings and elegant cursive, a truth or secret only available to another woman.

I searched the map and found that Lake 5 has cutthroat trout in it, or did twenty-two years ago in '96, and according to Peggy's notes, also had fish forty years ago in '78. Another survey has not been made since. We suspect there will still be trout living in Lake 5, but as we near the shore, the water comes alive with hundreds of thumb-sized and shiny black tadpoles. Caleb smiles. *There aren't going to be any fish in this lake.* He says it without regret; he says it with the same excitement with which he spoke about the goats. Trout were a memory held in the silt and survey.

Trout, or fish of any kind, are not native to these lakes, are in fact, rarely found in alpine lakes. When this landscape formed, after the pullback of the glaciers, the way up to the lakes was, and remains, as steep as the slope we walked to get here. Fish passage was not possible. Not even the wiliest trout could make the jumps and climbs necessary to reach these waters. So, the ecosystem of lakes, like Lake 5, supports a different kind of life. Amphibians mostly. Along with the other aquatic insects that standing water attracts. I asked Caleb how he knew, with such certainty, there would be no fish. He explains that the cutthroat would have eaten the tadpoles when they were young, smaller than they are now. Eventually, the fish would have depopulated the lake of frogs almost entirely. We begin a slow walk along the shore and I hear a splash, and then another—all around us, Columbia Spotted Frogs jump from their rock or log perches and bellyflop into the glass clear water.

We set up our tent among the tracks of cougar, deer, elk, bear, and what looks to be the narrow track of a small wolf. It will feel good to sleep on this earth where so many animals have stood. The mud that was a shallow pond only weeks ago holds each print as if cast in clay. As I trace the outline of the bear's toes the soil does not crumble beneath my finger. I can make out the lines of the pad of the bear's foot like the lines on the palm of my hand, and for a moment I am a palmist smiling at what I hope is a good, strong life line. I crawl to the next track. A cougar paw with a dip of a claw print. The doe had a fawn beside her, heart after heart of hoof tracks pressed into tan earth. The elk was moving quickly; it was the only track that showed any sign of a slide. It makes me happy to know that even as we walk atop them, our footprints will not cover theirs, will not destroy them, and will not even be traceable among them. Three days later, when we pack our tent to leave, the only sign of our being here will be a slight disruption of earth where we went in and out of the tent. Even this will be smoothed out with a pine bough.

As Caleb filters water from the lake, I walk its circumference. I am walking off a headache. That, combined with unwarranted underlying anxiety and breasts that mark each hard step with a pang of pain, are harbingers of my menses. I will bleed while we are here. I used to avoid hiking and backpacking altogether when I was menstruating. And for good reason. I get devilish cramps. Cramps that force me to lie down, to curl into a comma. And, because of a tipped uterus, my blood rarely comes in manageable doses, but often all at once, spilling from me in such a way that I must find a bathroom, a place to allow my body to drain.

But as I have become more accustomed to this landscape, more comfortable in it than not, and now that I know more about the people who inhabited this land and inhabit it still, I have found it very natural to come to the woods during my menses. Movement has always quelled the pain. Finding a rock or stump on which to sit while my uterus sheds its layers, while my body completes another cycle that female bodies, human and not, share, is somehow comforting, communing, easier than experiencing the same indoors, placated with a hot pad and ibuprofen. As I walk the lake, frogs launching with my every step, I wonder how many babies were born upon these shores. I wonder about other Native women, those from only a century before. Had any of them labored here? Did their birthing cries echo along the granite where now resounds the *wop-wop-wop* of helicopters? That I know so little about these first women and their lives bothers me. Then again, that they were able to live as they did for thousands of years, leaving barely any sign, is commendable. To know that my blood will disappear into the earth with theirs is a feeling somewhere in the proximity of comfort. It is the most natural offering I can give these mountains, those mothers.

Frog after frog alerts my coming. Each with a wonderfully awkward and ridiculously formless leap. The frogs are the size of my hand or smaller. Some sit by themselves others are in pairs or groups, as if they are couples or families even though such behavior is not part of frog lifestyle. These frogs do not know monogamy, only survival. Their brown is the brown of tree bark and lake bottom. They move through the water with a grace I long to follow. And eventually will.

After walking the acre or so around the lake, I take rest among the stems and leaves of the dogtooth violet that has already bloomed out. Caleb is on his own walk. Silence takes lead on this Wilderness stage. The dogs are concerning themselves with squirrels or smelling the piss of other animals. The sun is almost directly above us. Butterflies, mostly yellow, but some white and indecorous, drift like falling petals of sunlight through the air. I close my eyes and hold the scene in situ. And then as a cloud drifts, the silence leaves. I hear song. Barely audible at first, then growing. The music of frogs! A choir of croaking amphibians fills the basin around us. When Caleb returns, he is grinning. He wants to know if I heard them. I nod. He says he has never heard Columbia Spotted Frogs sing. He tells me he counted sixty frogs as he walked around the lake. I smile back. I had not counted anything at all.

We hang our food and leave the extra gear in the tent. We want to walk out to where the goats were and we want to see the other lakes. Caleb packs his fishing pole and a plastic case of lures. I have the map, water, and snacks for the dogs and me. From here the terrain will be rolling, an easy up and down. I feel the same kind of excitement the dogs exhibit in their wagging, alert bodies. I am eager to know this place, eager to touch the water in the other lakes, to see what, if anything, the lures bring. And likely I am full of hormones as well, that sudden burst I get a day or two before my bleeding starts. I welcome it. I am glad for the extra energy.

As we imagined they would be, the goats are gone from the meadow. Not even a track remains which causes us to second guess what we both know we saw. We walk through a series of small hanging valleys and cirque basins. On my right, steep hillsides lead to ridgelines. To my left, miles and miles of Wilderness, sometimes abruptly and other times gently, draining down. Down toward Elk Creek, down toward the Salmon River. Down to the Columbia and eventually the Pacific. So much begins right here.

The next lake, Lake 6, is barely a half mile away. It sits confidently among granite boulders and lichen-covered outcroppings, and, unlike Lake 5, which only hosted five or six trees on a prominence in the center of its u-shape, Lake 6 is lined with spruce, lodge pole, and tall, tall whitebark pine. The lakes call to me differently now that I know about the frogs. The cool blue of the lake tempts. The sun has reached its apex. We are hot, and a swim sounds divine. But as we get closer, we see that the water is shallow, the bottom muddy. I search the water for frogs. I am eager for the splashes, now that I know what they mean about the lake's health. I want to see the tadpoles moving like impossible giant sperm in the clear shallow water. But the shoreline is silent, the water still. We step carefully around the edges, dodging mud, not wanting to crush the delicate grass or cast a human print where one doesn't belong. Halfway around the lake, we stop. I unshoulder my pack and reach for the map. I put my finger on Lake 6. Written beside its drawn kidney shape, is the word: *Barren.*

Barren. The word echoes against the cliffs like a whispered accusation, a scarlet letter pinned to the heart of this lake. But beauty is its own defense: sun-lit wings of mayflies dance in rehearsed patterns above the water, the intricate tracks of thirsty goats, deer, and elk tell tales of life-sustaining visits, and a chorus of birdsong rises from the spruce that skirt the shore. How many other beings thrive in the unseen depths, in ecosystems unknown and unimaginable? This blue dream is a reflection of sky, this water clear as the earth's conscience – Lake 6 is filled with abundance. So, why was it condemned by two syllables? I sit down on the trunk of a fallen tree and say the word aloud. *I don't like that word*, Caleb says in return.

What expectations do we have for wild places? How do words, maps, and human enhancements change the way we place value on nature? When there is nothing that benefits the machinery of our culture, by which I mean when something is no longer commodifiable, cannot offer a product, or does not lend itself to our sport, why is it deemed to be no longer of worth? Why must our judgments extend past our desires to profit or produce? I think back to a conversation, months prior, maybe in May or early June, when fires burned near the town of Durango and a friend wrote *I can barely stand to watch. All my beautiful wilderness is destroyed.*

My. Beautiful. Wilderness. Destroyed.

The word "barren" was loaded: with judgment, with the assumption that nature's beauty hinges solely on its perceived productivity to humans, and with a sense of entitlement. The very notion that these wild places could or should belong to any of us deeply troubles me. It seems to contradict the ancient wisdom of our ancestors who understood that we belong *to* the land, not the other way around.

Perhaps this unease stems from witnessing the consequences of land ownership, both public and private. When we claim something as ours—be it a horse, five acres, or an entire lake—do we not assume the right to determine its fate? And in doing so, have we not stripped away the very wildness that first drew us in?

What happens when that land no longer serves our purpose? Who clings to an unproductive farm, continues to feed the old mare, or hikes to a fishless alpine lake? The answer, I suspect, lies in recognizing that true ownership is not about control, but about responsibility and reverence for the wildness that sustains us all.

That same month when fires burned through Southern Colorado, friends from Maryland came to visit us in McCall. We decided to go on one of my favorite hikes, a rolling, comfortable walk to Grassy Twin and Coffee Cup lakes. We came to a turn in the trail that offered spectacular views. Before us, Hard Creek drainage spilled its way through granite cliffs and dense firs. For a distance that would have taken days to travel, our eyes followed the silver of the stream until it spilled out into a meadow some 10 miles below. There was so much to imagine in this vastness, we were silent and awestruck. Framing this scene were charred tree trunks and barren ground, testaments to a fire that had swept through two years prior.

I turned to my friends and asked if they were disappointed.

Why, they wondered. *Because it has burned*, I answer.

I wanted to know if they were disappointed that the landscape wasn't green and lush. I wondered how the result of the fire affected their judgment. They shook their heads, *no*. I explained that I was upset over judgments made about the value, or even beauty of a place after a fire, that I was frustrated by people's expectations of beauty. About what they considered beautiful. Caleb added that the view we had would not have been possible without the burn.

This wasn't death; it was simply another stage of life's cycle. As we hiked on, the landscape became a mirror reflecting our preconceived notions of beauty. But amidst the charred remains, new life was emerging: the delicate green shoots of countless young aspen, a testament to the resilience and renewal that often follows fire. It was a reminder that beauty can be found everywhere and that beneath the surface, unseen and unimagined, life persists.

Caleb and I turn east to leave Lake 6, passing a small ring of rocks untouched by fire for years. Caleb remarks on the lack of recent use in this part of the Frank Church compared to other areas outside the Wilderness. *I guess no one comes back here anymore,* he says, kicking at a tin can rusted. In his words, I sense both an ease and a touch of regret. It echoes a question that had been on my mind all day: What value does a place hold for most Idahoans, for those of us who live and recreate here, if it doesn't offer the promise of game to hunt or fish to catch?

That night I could not sleep. The rush of hormones that comes before the blood has its downside. I lie awake reading for an hour or so, then slide out from under my sleeping bag, unzip the tent door, and step out onto the dry earth. The sky is a chaos of stars, the Milky Way a joyous white brushstroke across a blueblack sky. The moon is waning crescent with just enough light to guide me without a headlamp to a log where I can sit to pee. I look out toward the lake, toward our orange tent that sits on its shore, and I think of how much the three lives therein mean to me. My family. One man, two dogs. The latter which I know will not remain as long as the former, the unfairness of the length of dog lives out of my control. Nevertheless, they mean the world to Caleb and me. Plans are made around their ability to join us. We rarely go anywhere without them.

We had talked about kids when we first met. But we were almost forty then, almost fifty now. It is likely it will remain just the two of us, and whatever canine companions we rescue until one or the other of us passes. I think it is fair to say that we both felt a little sadness about this, certain that our kids would love to share these experiences with us, and would be as feral as we were when we were kids—even as we are now. But I am at a risky age for childbearing. My periods have become irregular, at night I wake soaked in my cotton nightgown. The shape of my body is changing ever so slightly. When I tell my older sister, who is never gentle about these things, she says, *Welcome to hell*. My mom, with a different, distant perspective, says I am entering the best years of my life. There is no definitive guide, my doctor will tell me. *It is different for every woman*. But whether Caleb and I want children, the choice to do so naturally soon will no longer be mine. I finish peeing and wipe myself. There is pink on the cotton toilet paper. The first hint of a cramp. I push on my uterus with the heel of my palm. I feel the warm blood leave me.

The next morning, we woke up early and walked in the general direction of Lake 7: FISH. It is easy to make our way without a path. A turn right would take us up the ridgeline, left and we would go down a steep slope with the unnamed waters toward Elk Creek, or we can walk straight ahead along this shelf of land that holds lakes like gemstones in the palm of a hand. We go forward.

Lake 7 proves as easy to reach as the others. The day before, from the top of the ridge above us, we watched two downy mountain goats and one kid stroll the shore. But today it is only us. None of these lakes are large by Idaho standards, only an easy ten- or fifteen-minute walk around each. When we reach Lake 7's edge, we immediately see its depth. Though the lakes are not far apart, each one seems to have its own personality, to offer something different to the visitor. Balls of goat hair stick to the limbs of Labrador tea that surround the lake. I pull one off and hold it to my nose and smell only early morning.

Last night's breeze swept out the smoke from this valley so that the clear blue of sky reflects uninhibited from the surface of Lake 7. We sit in the shade on the lake's shore, and I eat a snack while Caleb attaches a small lure, the size of a bean, to his line. How gently his big fingers work with the small, silver lure. How deftly they make the knots in the almost invisible filament, and how easily he zips that line into the water. In no time he has a bite and is reeling but loses the fish. Again, and again he casts, the barb crimped against the hook which makes the catching harder, but also the odds less likely of killing a fish. He finally reels one in, and I am waiting beside him, camera in hand. We have taken it upon ourselves to do a new lake survey. Make a new, updated map. He will send the photos to his colleagues at Idaho Fish and Game and keep copies for his records.

The trout is small, maybe eight inches, silver and pink. But something looks amiss. The fish's head is misshapen, too big for the body. I say this to Caleb. *Overpopulated*, he replies. And though this is unfortunate and their presence here in Lake 7 is not natural, we feel somehow happy for them. Excited to have caught the fish, to pull a survivor from the depths of the lake. Lake 7 was last stocked nearly twenty years ago. If the fish is about seven years old, which Caleb assumes she is, then she is the great- or great- great- grandchild of the 1989 stocking of one thousand cutthroat trout, perhaps greater yet. I watch the careful way Caleb holds the fish, which I have witnessed now maybe a hundred times. His gentleness with wild things, his tenderness. He immerses his hand back in the water and the fish glides easily away. We repeat the process all around the acre distance of the lake then return to where we started. We put on our packs and move toward Lake 8. It is still early in the day; we want to explore as much as we can.

As we walk, I think of the fish we left behind. I think of how quickly she, and other fish, have grabbed the lure. There's not enough food for them, Caleb had said, many of them will starve to death, he adds in the voice that is the scientist, but also their advocate. Months later he will tell me about a species of finch that has all but disappeared from their native alpine lake habitat. The larvae, he said, of the caddisfly gets eaten by the stocked trout before the finch can get to it. It was one of their main food sources, and once gone, so was the Rosy finch. And though my knowledge of these ecosystems is limited, I can only imagine what else has been changed by our human desire to create within these pools some sort of life that humans deem valuable. I feel the cramps like a fist clenching in my stomach. I find a log, lift my dress, sit, and press my hand into my uterus. Watch as carmine falls to pine needles, then onto earth. Deep red clots among bright red blood. The last time I saw my doctor, she said that I had about three percent of my eggs left. Those numbers dropped steeply the closer I got to my final menses. I look at the blood on the ground. Tadpoles. Frogs. Overpopulation. Rosy finch. Natural state. Unproductive. All these words run through my mind as blood drains from between my legs.

Lake 8 is labeled: Barren.

I would later say it was a feeling like I imagined a baptism to be. It was the high point of my summer, I would tell friends when I showed them the picture.

The first time we came to Lake 8, we paused only briefly without much exploration. We were eager to make our way to the lakes farther away. But we did not pass by without commentary. We were both delighted by its color (turquoise), the depth (unknowable), and the beauty (incomparable.) On the shore of Lake 8 were fireweed blooming and numbering in the hundreds. Granite—black, white, and sparkling with mica—with mica tumbled toward the north and west shores of the lake. A meadow, verdant and supple, lay like an offering at the east shore, and to the south, boulders played their way into the water, more fireweed coming up like purple prayers from the parish of soil the granite offered. Here, I thought, I could spend all my summer days. Here is where we should have pitched our tent. Here is the most beautiful place in the Wilderness, in Idaho, in the West. My world, in a moment, became us and the lake. Memory and knowledge of other places I loved fell from me as blooms fell from fireweed. I lost all agency and for a moment felt that if I sat long enough, roots may grow from the backs of my legs, I might find myself as natural to the landscape as the whitebark pine or the milk-colored goat. Caleb tied lure to filament and cast again and again, each time bringing back nothing but the unzipping of water as he pulled the lure through it. Not barren, I said. We can't label it that. He nodded and added non-fish bearing. I smiled. Satisfied, but not completely so. The prefix *non* still brings with it a sense of the negative, of not being enough. I searched for a better label and could not find one. The word made sense for science, but I am not a scientist.

We make our way to Lake 3 (FISH), by midafternoon. Lake 3, which lies at the bottom of a steep scree slope, offers neither fish nor frogs, but Caleb strips off his clothes and dives into the water with as much grace. As naturally as either. I am bleeding steadily by now. The cramps are not horrible, but uncomfortable, my energy waning, so I lay in the shade with the dogs, their panting a metronome to my dreaming.

Caleb told me that when they first started stocking the lakes, the trout were brought by mule in large, tin milk jugs. What was it like, I wondered, when the first trout entered the water? Tens of thousands of years these lakes had been without fish and then, as the jugs were tipped, the water was chaotic with silver flashes. This must have seemed a miracle to early biologists and sportsmen. To be able to put life where life had not before been. I think of my friend Jennifer, five months pregnant now, and holding her hand as we watched a fertilized egg being planted into her uterus by the steady hand and focused intention of her doctor. *As of right now,* the nurse said when the doctor stood to leave, *you are pregnant.* Jennifer grasped her belly. We smiled at each other, and all the way home talked about due dates and baby showers.

She didn't want to get her hopes up, afraid she might lose this one as she had others before, but Griffin stuck with her. She shows me pictures of ultrasounds, lets me hear his heartbeat.

So much like a woman's most intimate parts, I think again. Each lake an ovary sending its water—life—down each of these outlets. The drainage itself with ridges and deep cuts like an exquisite vagina. The hills like full hips, like perfect breasts, nippled peaks as if mother nature lay herself down over and over, upon the nothing that was the earth before her coming. Saying here, here use this body. And we have.

I turn to look at the lake just as Caleb emerges from the water. His skin glistens like the trout's. He is a deep brown from days hiking, running trails. The water runs off his shoulders and down the length of him, and I trace each drop with my eyes as they travel down his chest, pelvis, and long legs, then return to the body of water. He smiles at me, and I wonder if we should make love. Here on the shores of Lake 3. And what if I were to get pregnant? Would we tell our child that they were conceived on the banks of a lake with no name in non-fish bearing waters, the dogs and trees and birds and goats as our witnesses? Would they grow to know this state as natural, to expect frogs before fish? My wondering ends with a cramp that reminds me that even if I wasn't bleeding, the chances of a pregnancy are slim and risk high. I think about all the years of fertility behind me and the years of infertility in front. In many ways, it will be nice to be through with this monthly ritual. The stains, the pain, my earlier years of worrying about missing a pill. And yet. In those years I had a choice. I could stop the pill, have the IUD removed, have unprotected sex, and watch my belly grow. What choice, I wonder, have we given nature?

I stand and look into the depths of the Wilderness, into the acres and acres of land I have not experienced. I gaze at ridgelines, and treetops, into a vastness that blends into a word I know only as landscape, with a qualifier as simple as beautiful. Hundreds of unnamed lakes lie before me. Streams without fish. Cliffs with neither mountain goats nor big horn sheep. And in the same view, all these things do exist. This landscape, like my own body, is a narrative of possibility. How it is perceived is found in the words we choose to describe it. As I stand by Lake 3, one of the most sacred choices a woman is slowly draining from me. And when it is gone, how might I be perceived? Labeled? I shoulder my pack and we hike the steep hill up and over the saddle and back to Lake 8.

The picture I show friends looks like this: The top half is sky. A double-peaked granite mountainside, and a scattering of tall, steeple-like sub-alpine fir who all seem to be tumbling graciously toward the water that makes up the bottom half of the picture. Water, a shade of green best described as spring green, as that delicate green in a mother-of-pearl ring, as new green. It is a green that is trying to remain green while simultaneously reflecting sky, trees, and granite. As if the water is in love with the rocks and sky and roots that saunter toward it. In the foreground, the backside of a woman's body, standing hip-deep in the water. Hair long and black. Just the hint of the round of her breasts can be seen on either side of her smooth brown back. Arms extended as if welcoming home a lover she had not seen in years. Extended as if she is caught in a moment of rapture. Extended as if she has been released. Is free. Her shoulders strong. Waist narrow. Hips full. In moments the hands will come together in a prayer that she will issue with her body, my body, as I dive into the water.

Even now, months later, I look at the picture and I am there again. In Lake 8. That almost post-menstrual body. Moments after he takes the picture, Caleb joins me in the water. Swims out beside me, dives beneath the surface, and rises and says, *open your eyes while you're under.* I do. And what I see is endless. Is what fish, stocked forty years before must have seen. And it is not potential. Or lack. It is closer to miracle. Closer to a word that I don't know, we don't use often enough. Have not created or have forgotten. I watch sun reflect off the minerals floating in the water, imagine I am swimming in a gemstone. The edges of my body appear blurred and time slows as water unclears my vision. I stay under as long as my lungs allow. Searching for nothing. Hoping for nothing. Wanting nothing more than to be held in this state of weightlessness. This quiet. This womb of earth. When finally I emerge, Carhartt, our oldest dog is swimming beside me. Cisco follows on the shore. Caleb is within arm's reach. My blood and the last of my reproductive days are slowly draining from me, and yet I feel that I will walk out of this lake with more than I entered it with. I swallow the water on my lips and blink it into my eyes.

When we leave the next day, it is not without a feeling that I am leaving something behind. Not the two feathers, stuck into the ground at the edge of the dry flat where we ate our supper and shared our morning coffee, one Clarks nutcracker for Caleb, one magpie for me, which I found as we hiked. Not gear or some random thing dropped. The map is safe, folded together with a larger map of the whole forest, tucked in my pack along with uneaten food and damp clothes, its words unforgotten but for now innocuous among all else that I carry. I feel no regret for not pulling fish from the lake to eat or bring home or pocketing this rock or that to place in the bowl of forest souvenirs that serves as a talking piece on our coffee table. It was something else. Something left without regret. Like information that no longer serves or a chance that you didn't miss taking.

As we make our way up the steep slope, I look back to the mud flat. The frogs, the tadpoles, the feathers left to twist in the wind—

none of that can be seen. From this height and this distance, the tracks of the deer and her fawn, the blue of mountain gentian, the blood, it is all part of a landscape. And the place where we had put our tent is better for our leaving, though I hope some of our dreams, or gratitude might linger, might be felt by whoever lay there next. I close my eyes and feel the low cramp in my belly that for 35 years has reminded me of the great possibilities of my body. I look back to where we have been. I see again the sparkling underwater of Lake 8 and remember what it was like to break through the surface, for my eyes to focus on the face of Caleb, hear Carhartt beside me, Cisco panting on the shore, and my own breath as I renewed it. The feeling of aliveness, joy, satisfaction. It is this feeling, this state of being that I still search to find a word for. I turn and look up the hill and see Caleb and the dogs waiting for me. Soon the lake and the goats and the fish will be memories which I will carry in my body. Directions for how to go on. A map to a landscape where I, too, am now drawn.

Resound

There may have been a No Trespassing sign, but we never saw it. The snow on that February day in central Idaho was over four feet deep. Any signs hung on barbed-wire or wooden fence posts painted orange were buried under five months of freeze.

We had begun on the road with our skis gliding comfortably in tracks left by snowmobiles. But we wanted off the road. We were fearful for our two dogs. Rumor was, around town, that a young man had set leg traps along the West Mountain Road, this road. So as soon as the tracks rose out and up to the meadow we stepped out and onto the untouched snow, cutting our own path into the field. The dogs, eager to explore, ran ahead but were not able to stay atop the soft crust and could gain no purchase. Reluctantly, they filed in between Caleb and me, walking easily on the hardpack his weight created.

The day had begun with the promise of bluebird skies and brilliant sun. Slowly clouds started stealing in from the northeast, gathering at Council Mountain and threatening more weather. All weekend we had watched the storms come and go, sometimes dropping as much as an inch of snow an hour, other times pelting our roof with graupel. It had been an unsettled February.

We fell easily into the rhythm of our exercise. The lenitive *swish swish* of skis in tandem was the sound that carried us over what would be, in summer, lush grazing for black-faced cattle, maybe red Herefords, or a field-nesting, yellow-breasted meadowlark—animals and colors unimaginable in this, the deepest of our winter months. The most temporary of blue sky offered hope from a palette dichromatic, merely white and brown; even the needles of pine on the foothills before us were frost-covered and gray. When I first moved to Idaho seven years earlier, this white, this silence, was damning. I spent the winter months feeling trapped by weather, longing for my feet on bare earth. Driving south, when weather permitted, in hopes of seeing green, seeing yellow arrowleaf balsamroot in the canyons near Boise, hearing water rush in the north fork of the Payette. But I had fallen in love. With spring-fed mountain freshets, with the golden-beaked tanager that came to our feeder, with the wild and sweet huckleberries, and dashing crimson paintbrush, and the robin trilling her morning song, the bugle of the elk, and nights in the Wilderness north of us when the air was graced with the long, holy melody of wolves in the midnight. And the larch. The larch becoming flame on the hillside, the surrender of summer, the cant of light in autumn pushing warmth through the boughs as the rivers returned to lower flows. The first snow became the sigh that brought us into our cabin, into rest. The quiet calms us as it does the hibernating bear, and the rattlesnakes in their den. There is beauty here which could only be recognized when I accepted each season as part of the whole. What this deep moisture feeds are the palette and chorus of summer. When I look to the miles of deep white snow, across the pasture, and up the mountain side, I know the dream of the lily-petaled trillium beneath, the thimbleberry that will stain my tongue in August.

Yet winter at this high elevation can be deadly. The deep snows can become a trap for both fawns and elk calves born late in the summer, as well as full-grown ungulates that find themselves stuck in chest-deep drifts unable to outrun a predator or starved by moisture that buries graze. In McCall, the town we live in, families of mule deer and a variety of fox have come to depend on handouts to keep them alive at an elevation they might otherwise need to descend from, but this generosity doesn't reach the rural landscapes, proof of which lies in front of us in a circle of fur and hooves, and pink droplets of fresh blood that have melted and stained the snow.

The doe was likely a yearling. Its deathbed is surrounded by the tracks and scat of a variety of birds and mammals: coyote, magpie, raven, and perhaps, it seems, a mink. Likely it was a wolf who brought the doe down, but perhaps she was already stuck, and the canine visitation was one of relief—a quicker death than starvation. We bend to the scene with the interest of biologists, or perhaps it is more like sociologists, learning to understand this wild society and appreciating it in its natural sense. There was something easy in the deer's repose as it lay as an offering in a place where these things make sense. The ingesting of one life to sustain others. I have watched osprey take fish from a high mountain lake, and once, a bald eagle snatch a grown goose from the sky above the Snake River, and though both were difficult to witness, I could not begrudge animals I revere for doing what they do to survive. All I love in this vast and wild landscape includes a substantial amount of appropriate death.

We rise from the scene and continue to ski toward the tree line. Caleb veers east recalling an abandoned homestead he had heard about from a colleague. We glance at the horizon and find the telltale stand of trees foreign to the cleared meadowland. It is near, a mile or less, and we increase our strides with an eagerness, our imaginations working on the same ideas, but in silence.

The house is typical of the 1920s or '30s. Faded white, sharp-roofed, modest, with a touch of fancy in the decorative trim on the awnings, the porch extending into the snow. Three cottonwoods stand as sentinels in the yard, seventy, maybe eighty years in their rings, and from the limb of the tallest, a rope is taut into the snow, suggesting a black Goodyear somewhere in the frozen white beneath. I smile at the scene. The house looks like it was picked from a Sears and Roebuck catalog, just as my dad's Montana home was, delivered by train and moved by horses to a place not far from the tracks. I search the yard for the lilacs that would complete the picture and find their brown fingers reaching from snow to sky, roots asleep in the dream of purple. Soon we see the tops of an occasional fencepost, a barrier serving no purpose for at least half the year, but nevertheless, we enter the yard where we imagine a gate to be. I expect that any moment a dog, not unlike one of our own, will come bounding toward us as warning and welcome. Carhartt and Cisco, perhaps sensing the same, move eagerly toward the house, ears pricked, the younger dog's tail busy.

The house is so confidently placed in this stand and camouflaged by color that it takes me some time to realize that the snow is banked against the beveled siding, in some places only three feet deep, in other places up to the first-floor windowsills. The doors are forced into their jams, impossible to open outward. I wonder how the family managed the winters. The work of shoveling was made twice as hard by the wind that would constantly move snow, like waves, to fill in paths cut from kitchen to outhouse, from mudroom to barn. I find myself admiring the kind of peace that might bring, not being able to get out. I'm romanticizing. But as we near, the fantasy skews. The large picture window that in summer framed a meadow, is broken. The snow has pushed through and made a ramp into the living room.

I sit on the back of my skis and look in. Carhartt, the eldest dog, the one more prone to adventure, sits beside me, eager to enter. The slope of snow is inviting. In a simple move, I might crouch, shift forward my weight, and ski right into the domesticity before me. The room is a mix of twin recliners, a rust-colored sofa, end tables, and lamps. An empty fireplace, by simply existing, adds warmth. I unclip my skis and leave them at the entrance, perhaps out of decorum, and scooch carefully into the living room. I lower the zipper of my jacket, stuff my wool hat in my pocket, and fall into the desire to explore which often overwhelms my common sense.

Many of Caleb and my adventures find us drawn to places like this. We hike to abandoned mines, decommissioned fire lookouts, and forgotten ghost towns. We like to reimagine lives in these places. To wonder at the hopes and hardships of Native people and those who later homesteaded in these valleys, built shacks near their claims, or created entire towns banking on a windfall from the railroad that they were certain was to come. There are always clues to their personalities that exist now as ghosts. A forgotten Reader's Digest found on the floor of a low-roofed shack near the Deadwood mine. An ornate bedstead leaning against equally lavish wallpaper peeling from the wood in an upstairs room of a deserted hotel. And in Southern Utah, a toy pistol rusted and weathered in a dry streambed not far from a ramshackle lean-to. I am especially fond of an old photograph we came upon last summer near the Snowshoe Mine in the Frank Church Wilderness. It was lying on a rough-hewn countertop among rat droppings and coffee cans of rusted nails. The person in the photo was too faded to distinguish, but the lean of the body, the raised hand, hinted toward an intimacy not intended for us. We set it back on the shelf as we had found it, knowing that both the photographer and the photographed were long dead and would be, at least in this photo, forever unnamed. Farther down the road and near Crooked Creek we found the remains of an old schoolhouse. The choice location was poor and the flooding creek had filled the single room where the daughters and sons of the miners and their wives learned their numbers and recited the Pledge of Allegiance. In the corner, an old woodstove stood on thick iron legs, its door open and the ash from a years ago fire was buried beneath a nest of some sort. I imagine the life both woodstove and schoolhouse once held. The easy laughter of children. The strange safety this school in the Wilderness provided as their fathers burrowed clumsy holes in the earth and their mothers cut patches of rhubarb for pies. The children who learned there could be great grandparents now, but it is more likely the only thing surviving from this Wilderness schoolhouse are handed-down stories and a smooth brass knob on a door forever held open by mud.

I run my fingers along the tassels of a green and brown crocheted afghan that hangs on the back of a tan recliner and wander into the kitchen. There I find the ubiquitous white refrigerator of the late 1950s and its matching stove. Cans of food still line the pantry shelves, the familiar Van de Camp's pork and beans, soup, and several other cans with labels missing. The white porcelain basin of the deep kitchen sink is filled with dishes carefully stacked. It's hard to tell if the thin plates were dirty when the occupants left or if time has made them so. I stand at the sink and look out the window toward No Business Mountain. How many other women did this over the last seventy-five years? Looking toward the trees, searching the pasture for cattle and kids, taking a reprieve from her tasks to imagine the tops of mountains or life in town, before returning to the dishes, or the rhubarb pie baking in the oven. Out of habit, out of practice, I wipe my gloved hands on the towel that hangs from the oven door, careful to straighten it and smooth the word *Sunday* which is hand-embroidered along with pink and orange and blue wildflowers.

From the kitchen, I go to a later addition, a bathroom, the plumbing exposed, almost like an embarrassment. The toilet is secure, but the floorboards rot behind it. There is an attempt at a shower. Craftsmanship is lacking here, unlike the rest of the house. I am uninterested and leave, crossing again through the front room, through the mudroom, seeking stairs to the room above. Carhartt is beside me as I carefully test each step before giving it my full weight. I hold the painted handrail to my left and almost call to Caleb that we are going up, but instead, silently ascend. The smell of pack rat greets me in the stairwell, nails extend from the wall where pictures once hung.

We reach the top and find only one room. Like the rest of the house, it is painted white, which has aged to an icteric yellow. The ceiling slopes so steeply that I must move to the middle of the room to stand erect. The bed, a twin, the kind with a brown metal headboard and exposed springs is pushed to the wall. The mattress is blue-striped and stained and there is a hole where the rats have gnawed their way in. I press my hand against the tick and and push. The springs squeak a memory of climbing into my own childhood bed. A colorfully woven rug lies perfectly flat next to the bed in a way that beckons rest despite the unsanitary accommodations. I turn to the dresser that stands against the same wall as the open door. It is the only unpainted wood I've seen in the house. I grasp the handle and pull open one drawer to find rat droppings, then another to find a red t-shirt, neatly folded. In the corner, a pile of clothes is heaped, and looks like a crouched child in an eternal game of hide-and-seek. I touch it with my toe, but only the dust moves. The room holds no closet, only a hook nailed to a wall where nothing hangs. At the peak of the roof, there is a small window and I walk toward it. Outside the wind has started blowing, flakes push against the pane. What a comfort this home must have been to its inhabitants when compared to the chaos outside. We, however, will be skiing out in a storm.

Carhartt and I descend the stairs. When we reach the landing, I pause in the mudroom, an addition made by enclosing the back porch. In my grandmother's home, this is where the toys were stored. There is a rocking chair for morning coffee and sunrises, and windows lining the entirety. I spot a stack of books and bend to glance at the titles. They are not typical of the reads I usually find in abandoned places. Instead of bawdy covers promising romance, or Stetsoned men seeking vengeance, I find a copy of Abbey's *Monkey Wrench Gang* and a collection of Wallace Stegner titles that sit on my own shelf. I sit down on the floor and inspect another stack. I recognize the gilded spines of Little Golden Books and the felicitous covers of the *Little House on the Prairie* series. I sit down on the floor and begin to skim the pages, nostalgia or a feeling of knowing sweeps over me. Did the child that grew here feel a kinship to little Laura Ingles? Was she, like me, a shy young girl who got lost in books, whose best friend was a dog, whose imagination built for her a world of adventure, and who every day hoped it was the last day of school so that she might be free from learning and turned out under the big summer sky? I am quick to imagine my own life in this history, to seek kindred ghosts. Excited for the other titles, I lift a stack from the box and reveal the shiny brass of spent bullet casings instead.

.308? .306? I don't read the caliber, even though I am familiar with both. Guns were as common as the books in my childhood home. I was raised by ranch folks. I was gifted a BB gun for my ninth birthday and a rifle when I was old enough to hunt. I was captain of my college pistol team, a time when the sound of brass casings jingling in my pocket was more likely than loose change. The sound of pistol or rifle fire once signaled the end of a hunt or another match won.

But now, the sharp crack of gunfire echoes with a different meaning, unsettling and jarring. I drop the books and rise to my feet. Outside the sky is darkening, and the walls of the house moan against the winter wind. I spy another casing and no longer trust the floorboards. I look out of the window for Caleb and Cisco, and when I don't see them, I call out. I try to open the door knowing the drifts outside, then walk past the windows that look like old slides, each frame white, each latch closed, until I reach the last whose glass is a series of concentric cracks. There, in the middle of the pane, a single bullet hole. I bring my face close to the glass, my cheek feeling the cold, and look through the small hole in the center as if looking through the scope of a rifle. The pane is intact, but the impact had caused it to rupture into an ever-growing spider web pattern so that when I begin to move away from the bullet hole, the tree outside, the frozen swing, the snow-covered pasture, and gray sky are all fractured pieces of themselves, repeated again and again in irregular fragments of once perfect glass. The sound of that shot must have frightened, echoed up the stairs into the bedroom. Flushed birds from the trees. I try not to hear it, but I do. I hear it over and over again.

I look for Carhartt, but she is gone. My gloved finger is tracing the edge of the bullet hole when Caleb calls to me. He is bent at the window I slid through, looking in. He asks if I am okay and I tell him about the casings and the bullet hole. "We should go," he replies. I walk to the living room window and reach for his hand and he pulls me out. I hurry into my skis and we follow our tracks out. Past the cottonwood trees and the lilac, over the unseen fence, and toward the road we left. I pause only to put my hat back on and zip my jacket. I do not look back. The wind is spinning the powder in every direction now. In a couple of hours, all traces of our being here will be erased by wind and covered in snow. The house will again be buried in winter silence, save for the moan of the storm and the sound of pack rats scurrying across the bedroom floor.

Letter Born of a Snowy Morning

I have a mind of snow, but a heart of spring.

It seems today may be the day the sun breaks finally through the foam of clouds like a Steelhead breeching from icy depths. Yesterday, another six inches of snow fell on these Salmon River Mountains. This morning, filling the kettle, I marveled at the snow several inches up the kitchen window. I am surrounded by water and yet, do not drown. I look above the snow, to the forest beyond our cabin and try to imagine a different scene, one not dichromatic. When the limbs of pines were not heavy with snow and the transplanted rhubarb, now nearly six feet below this winter white, was leafy and green. I turn the kettle on to boil and though I know better, I think there is no way all this snow will ever melt, can ever be gone from our woods, will never not be enough.

But the sun is writing the truth on the landscape and the birds deliver the lines to the air. And this should be evidence enough. But we keep turning to other sources, sources outside ourselves and nature for proof. As if this truth can be found by a search engine as if it needs to be spoken in our language. The lines of this morning's poem are written in a vocabulary we have forgotten, an instinct we no longer trust, an inward search rarely taken. They are written for a world yet created, known by all our ancestors, and with an intelligence we have yet to achieve.

Though Saturdays, for me, are usually filled with much of the domestic, I pushed chores aside and sat in my reading chair and watched the weather come. It was so like a spring storm! Blizzard of fine snow, then flakes the size of a squirrel's fist, then graupel, then sun. All the while the birds feasted on seeds in the feeders and then on the seeds that blew to the ground. Like messages from the day's imagination, the birds came. Dark-eyed Juncos, Mountain and Black-Capped Chickadees, Red-breasted Nuthatches—and the bigger birds, too—Flicker, Steller's Jay, and Downy. And despite the wind and snow and cold, they sang and chattered. Maybe not despite it all, maybe it was because of it all they sang.

Funny, isn't it, how we have come to talk about the weather. Around town, people are cursing the snow and the pattern of storm upon storm and the gray days they bring. They long for weather that suits their needs, whatever those may be, or perhaps they're just ready to put the heavy coats and broad shovels away. Just yesterday, while I was brushing the truck off for a trip to town, a neighbor pulled up next to me and said, "This fucking snow. I've had enough of it." I must tell you, I winced. His anger, though directed at the weather, felt personal. But I've been there. There is a work to winter that sometimes feels an inconvenience to our human expectation of ease, and there have been times when brushing or scraping the windshield, shoveling the driveway, or being denied a visit because of bad roads has caused me contempt toward the weather as well. But that's changing. Last spring, I learned from Haida culture that to curse the weather is to offend it, is to not trust something far wiser and ultimately far more powerful than me. So, like the beings with whom I share this place, I now thank the weather or say nothing at all. Sometimes, I find myself apologizing, for it can be argued that we and our ways have influenced the weather, changed or altered its behavior. This, above all, should be a stronger argument against cursing it. When Samuel L. Clemmons wrote, "Everyone complains about the weather, but no one does a thing about it," he was talking about one thing. Now it means something entirely different.

The snow is so deep, the neighbor's cabin can no longer be seen and the youngest pines in our mixed conifer forest are completely covered.

I almost wrote "buried" instead of covered, but there is nothing dead about the scene. I like to think of the cold and white that covers the small trees as a quilt with a batting of winter that knows how to tuck a young pine in. I imagine what those saplings feel as the snow becomes their air and sky and when winter finally covers our kitchen window, I might know. Well, it will be an abstract knowing, as I need these walls as protection. Yet the comfort of this snow is something I think I do understand.

My partner Caleb calls this Salmon Weather, and I have started calling the snowstorms Salmon Weather also, and the snow, Salmon Snow. I love that name, it alludes to insurance, but also to a future I'm hoping will arrive. Here, at 6000 feet, the snow is deep and will linger until June, but up higher, in the places where winter is a song sung even on summer mornings, the snow can hold out 'til July and August, a snow reservoir, melting slowly, releasing water to streams, which flow into rivers. This cold runoff will come when the rivers are at their lowest and warmest when Salmon are returning, when most fish are spawning, when water, preferably cool water, is what these fishes need most. Another term I love: cold water refugia. What poet wouldn't love such a phrase; what mortal sinner could resist the word "refugia?"

Refugium, refugia, Latin for refuge, for hideaway. The words deliver a sense of relief, elicit a memory of safety, or at least the expectation of some kind of temporary amnesty—a rest. The forest has often been my refuge. The wild places, the copse of trees or a mountain lake a shelter from the conditions of human living, a safe place, too, like the arms of a good mother or accepting lover, or the deep belly fur of my old dog where I bury my face and cry for the years we've had, the months we have left. Cold water refugia is all this, but on a piscine level. In rivers, refugia can come in the form of upwellings, can flow from the mouths of streams, can exist in the shade of bankside trees. Rest areas for

Salmon and Steelhead making the long trip home—equally necessary for aquatic dwellers seeking relief from rising river temperatures.

It's arduous enough, the nearly 700 miles some Salmon will travel from the Pacific to Stolle Meadows, their birthplace, and that, too, of the South Fork of the Salmon River, where they will spawn. They begin the trip about now and will arrive sometime in July—during the hottest time of the year. To know summer on the South Fork I spent a week, not far from Stolle Meadows, backpacking along her shore. The temperatures were in excess of 100 degrees. My companions and I would rise early to walk in the coolest part of the day, and at night we would sleep on top of our bags, wishing the stars were rain, wishing for the slightest breeze to cool our skins. During the day we took our books and lunches and bunched in a narrow stream drainage, where we kept our feet in the water, cooled our heads under a short pour-off, and soaked our hats and clothes in the cooler water of Fritzer Creek, only to have all of it parched in an hour.

The winter before had been a dry one. There were fires throughout the west and smoke was our unfortunate companion and only seemed to intensify the heat. It was on that July backpacking trip, working the nozzle of my water filter between rocks, that I saw the first dead Sculpin. I turned to my friend, a fisheries biologist, who stood a few feet behind me, just as she noticed the dead fish. I watched as a look of shocked sadness and then exasperation passed like a cloud across her face. She pointed a finger longer than the fish itself, a being who despite their constancy in the river, stayed hidden, camouflaged, pressed against the river bottom without a bladder to give it buoyancy, and said, *they are the river's thermometers*. Seeking a reading we would understand, we tied my backpack thermometer to a length of fishing line and sunk it in the water. A few minutes later, when we pulled it out, the reading was in the 70s. My friend got on her knees at the water's edge, saying over and over, *hot, it's too hot, too hot*, and shook her head as she looked into the water. Her stare dove past the reflection of sky, past what riffles remained, past the layer of thick, warm water, to the thin, only slightly cooler water below. She looked for Salmon, not just with the eyes of a scientist, but with the look of a child who knew that something was wrong and that somehow they'd played a part in it. It's a look of regret and apology, one I've seen in the face of so many beloveds when they felt they were the cause of some hurt, some agony, be it from accidentally spilling their milk to the moment just after killing a deer. It's a look that says *My god, what have I done?* Salmon cannot survive in a river with a temperature in the 70s.

Is prayer a refugia? Though here I think it is important to point out the subtle difference between refugia and refuge, as subtle differences matter to the former. Whereas refuge as defined in *Webster's Ninth New Collegiate Dictionary*, is "A place that provides shelter or protection from danger or distress" or "Something to which one has recourse in difficulty," Refugia, in contrast, is defined as "a geographical region that has remained unaltered by a climatic change (such as glaciation) affecting surrounding regions and that therefore forms a haven for relict fauna and flora." What gives me pause in refugia's definition is the juxtaposition of "climatic change" and "haven", but the word that stops me altogether is "relict" which adjectively means widowed, but whose noun form represents plant and animal species living in isolation in small, localized area as survivors from an earlier period, or as what's left of a nearly extinct group. My heart wanders to another friend who is with us, whose ancestors fished Salmon from this river for thousands of years. I hear their voices in her prayers and stories. If it is the words that land between hands or are cast on water when we fear the losing of something loved, something beloved, of life itself, then prayer is merely a refuge, and the refugia we beg is in the hands themselves. I lift the marooned Sculpin from the sand and carry it into deeper water. I place my cupped hands in the river, then open them. The Sculpin sinks immediately from my view, its work done, as if the river itself had sent a plea, a prayer to the feeble gods who have some power to save. As if it is trying to empower us with a different godliness, as if the river has hope. Hope in, of all things, us.

Today there is neither an abundance of heat nor sunshine. It's been weeks of gray and it's not so much the snow anymore as the moroseness that has settled in. I have been reckless, as of late, attaching my emotions to seasons. Thinking I would be happier if I just held out for change. I recall a bouquet of tulips sent by my late husband and a card that read, "Hold on. Spring is coming." But with it, I became a relict myself. When I needed shelter from the pain of losing him, I went to the winter memories and found it. What bliss in naivete, but who could have known, and how would I have changed the outcome when it is only my reactions I control? There is science that proves the need for sun to lift the spirits, but there's science, too, that proves perspective is power. Rather than waiting for the warmer days that eventually I, too, will want relief from, I am becoming nonjudgmental of the weather and more interested in experiencing the days as they come, aligning myself with the will of the weather, moving through my days purposefully, trying to learn the song I am meant to sing, the one that carries tones of love, fear, regret, and apathy, in its lines, the one that defines me as human, just as the newly arrived Cassin's Finches and Robin sing songs belonging just to them. Let it be that, then, that brings me joy, the simple act of being, and not what I attach to it. Let it be the birds themselves who I will miss, should they never again return, and not that which I have projected on them, not a burden that is not theirs to carry. Let it be the Salmon I am thinking of when I see the snow, let it be their convenience I am praying for, not mine. Help me remember that the promise of a better future lies in my actions, not theirs.

Two weeks ago, Caleb, the dogs, and I went down the mountain to Hells Canyon. We went to greet the season. To touch the skin of the earth, to see the colors the canyon held, and to hear the voices carried on her winds. On a sunny morning, we decided to take a walk along the Snake River, below Hells Canyon Dam. It felt good to see the multiplicity of colors. There were purple Shooting Stars and yellow Meadow Buttercup. The green of the moss that clung to the granite was the mother of the green that was worn by the Maidenhair Fern. On the rocky cliffs across the river, we spotted what looked like piles of snow but were piles of white fur on the thick bodies of Mountain Goat. I removed my winter layers and let the sun bring out my colors, too. I followed the blue line of water to where it led to the mouth of the canyon and there sunlight spilled across the water, binding the surface so for a moment seemed like a silver trail we could walk. Blue were the lines that were riffles around rock. Blue was the sky where it met the walls of the gorge which rose unbelievably high. Green was the pine that was staggered intermittently, sojourners on this self-same walk. And in the distance, the Seven Devils and blanketing their flanks and horns, more white snow. Mountains and mountains of snow. There is the season we seek. There, in the mind of winter, where the language of summer, for fishes and others, is spoken by the falling of snow. The story they carry is ancient, and the message is always the same. Here is the refuge, the refugia, the water says to Salmon, and to us, here is the hope you seek.

The snow has started again in earnest. Little fists of snow. Snow like kisses blown in the air and frozen. Snow in clumps as big as some of the smallest Chickadees. Snow that with a little more sun will begin to melt, and whose water, as if desperate to return to its source, will start the journey down. Maybe some of this snow that I have watched all season will make its way to the Snake River. The melt will flow past the place where my family and I walked, past where runoff seeped from a granite wall, where I pressed my face against moss until my nose and cheeks were so cold they hurt. Past the place where after we turned away from the snow-packed mountains, turned back toward the dam, I saw the silver semi backing down to the river, its belly full of young Salmon, its presence shadowed by the very contraption that created it. It backed up, and a hose was placed in the water and a valve opened and thousands of young fish entered the river. I tried to find them in the current, but the river is a good mother, she covered her own, and all I could see was cold water, only water. Just like now, only snow. So much snow it seems that there has always been and will forever be snow. And though it does not seem possible, I no longer seem to mind. Maybe the river's desires have also become mine. for if rivers could hope, this would be theirs.

No Way to Say Goodbye

We are standing on the downstream bank of the Selway River on the border between Montana and Idaho. Monday morning, July 26th, 2019. We woke only two hours earlier at Paradise Campground, a mile or so away, in Montana. What was supposed to be a hot night turned out to be clear and cold, and several times I wrestled with my sleeping bag and the dogs as they pinned one corner or another of it down, leaving my shoulders or feet exposed. Your head was next to mine on the pillow, asleep minutes after you put it there. As is usual, I took upwards of an hour to fall asleep and gazed through the back window of the truck's camper shell at stars so abundant I had to put my glasses back on to be sure I was seeing each independently, not as duplicates.

Your oldest friend, Joe, and his brother, Chris, had scored a late-season pass to float the Selway, and though you wrestled with whether or not to go, you finally said yes. I wonder if the struggle was because of my history with kayaks and rivers or the fear of the words I would say to you at the put-in—the words I had said once before—another trip, another river, different friends.

Please don't die.

I rehearse the words before I say them to you. I am practicing the speech I will give you and your friends about no booze and boating, no fucking around, portage when you are uncertain. As you are each packing your boats, I finally say, "Make good choices." I do not tell any of you to have fun or be safe or take pictures.

While you pack, I walk to the sign at the trailhead that follows the river for forty-seven miles to Selway Falls, where I will meet you in three days. On the message board, alongside a poster of Smokey Bear, photos of noxious weeds, and a reminder to "pack it in/pack it out," is a picture of two brothers. It reads Missing Since May 2018.

I had seen the picture of the brothers months earlier driving to Moscow, Idaho, along the Clearwater River. A billboard along the roadside. They are both in camouflage, smiling. They are shoulder to shoulder. The tip of a deer antler is showing near one brother's knee. They have no idea that in a matter of months or days—I do not know when the picture was taken—they will be in a car that slides off the road we drove to get here, just a short way upstream of where we stand, and end up in Deep Creek and eventually the Selway. Two men will escape and swim to safety, two more will perish in the car, and the two brothers will remain unfound for what is now fourteen months.

We all talked about this as we drove to our campsite at Paradise. We wondered where the vehicle slid from the road, how high the spring runoff was, how it would happen that both brothers would have gotten lost in the water together, how they could still remain unfound.

Returning to the put-in, I say to you, the fish biologist who has packed snorkeling gear, "I think you might find them." The river is low. You are on the search and rescue team in our home county, and I am trying to soothe myself with words. I am trying to change the narrative. You smile at me, also believing it possible. The river is very low. No rain. The snow is mostly down from Trapper Peak and the other high mountains that feed the river.

Casually, I say, "Look for bones."

Joe tilts his head, says, "That's pretty awful."

"Those families need closure," I say.

In my mind, I see a log jam with a tear of camouflage fabric. I see a candle next to a photo of a smiling man, beside it a wife wanting to bury something other than her face in her hands. She is done believing that they somehow escaped. She wants to put herself and his body to rest. Let a little dust come to the silver frame.

I say this, and I see a yellow helmet in a spring river. Wyoming. The Clark's Fork. Fifteen years earlier. The helmet goes up and down in the rapids. "He was monkeyed up on a rock," Jim said. I thought that meant sitting on top of it. I thought that meant alive. No, you would tell me later. It meant that the water had forced Randy up against a rock, a rock I have never seen nor ever looked for, but I imagine as the size of an armchair, black with lichen, gray on top because it is dry, dry enough for Randy, my husband, on June 26th, 2004, to put his bare hands on and pull himself up.

I push Jim. I yell at him. "How could you leave him?" We are standing on a road near Painter's Bridge. Clark County, Wyoming. I had gone inside the store across the highway to buy snacks or beer or maybe to use the bathroom. I was going to meet Randy and Jim at the takeout. They were going to be there any minute. But a woman ran in just as I was checking out. Said that someone had fallen in the river. I said to the cashier, "My husband is a medivac pilot. He will find them." But monkeyed up on a rock didn't mean safe. You will tell me that by the time Jim saw Randy against that rock, Randy was probably dead.

When the tip of your boat barely touched the Selway, I told you that I wished you had a helmet that was a color other than black. A bright color. Something easy to spot in case you came out of your boat. You pointed to the water and gave me that look. I could see the bottom. The day before, we had walked into the middle of it. We felt the cool water on our feet, then ankles. Only when I neared a debris jam did it get as high as my knees. I reached both hands down and pulled up my skirt, laughing. This was how I counted coup with rivers. Standing in their middle, my feet solid on their rocks, this was how I took my story back. This was how I forgave water. I waded back to you and pointed to a stonefly. It was the color of fall grass—long, delicate. Its antennae were still searching in the wind. I reached down to pick it up and asked if it would bite. No, you told me, it was only the exoskeleton. I took it from the rock, held it in my hand, and wondered how something so lifelike could be hollow. A breeze lifted it from my palm and carried it to the water, where I watched it ride the riffles until I could not see it anymore.

You have often said that water is unforgiving yet continue to kayak. You take long runs and backpack alone into the forest, into the Frank Church Wilderness whose boundary is near our home. "If I break a leg or get heat exhaustion, I have a pretty good chance of making it." I imagine I am lying next to you in bed as you are telling me this, but it is just as likely that we are standing in the kitchen or driving or you are giving me an argument as to why you won't wear a Spot, don't need to check in. You say in nature you don't want to feel restrained. I don't say that your carefree thinking comes at the cost of mine.

I want to tell you I find your lack of concern for me disrespectful, and irresponsible, knowing my history. How, for the first couple of years, I will pace the living room of our cabin, how I will go to bed, get back up, eat ice cream, drink wine, go to bed again, then take Nyquil or Advil PM so I can sleep, so that I am awake just enough to say goodnight when finally you do come home, just awake enough to ask you to take a shower before getting in bed. I will then roll over, my back to you, and go to sleep hugging my pillow and telling myself that maybe you need to find someone who can go on these long runs and hikes with you. That a woman more like yourself would be a better match for you than I am—someone who can keep up. I tell myself I need to find a man who doesn't take these chances. Fuck you, I will scream to both you and Randy in my head. Fuck you both for taking these chances with me. But by morning, my fear and anger will subside.

I will ask you about the scenery, ask if you saw any animals. Did you take pictures?

The morning before Randy drowned in the Clark's Fork River near Painter's Bridge in Wyoming, he and I went for a walk. We were camping with Katie and Buster, two of our four dogs. When we reached the top of a small ridge, Randy sat on a boulder, looked toward the river, and I snapped a picture. He is wearing a light blue polo, jeans, a ball cap, and his favorite sunglasses. This picture would be the last picture ever taken of him. He is looking away from me. Or so it seems, but perhaps his dark lenses hide his true gaze. For years, I will wonder if he is saying goodbye. His hands were shaking at breakfast. He said he was nervous but did not know why. The picture sits on my desk at home. A brown frame that is supposed to look like natural wood but isn't. A simple 4x6 that now I cannot even remember having developed. It must have been so hard to open that envelope of pictures. To see him again, alive and sitting on that rock, with the pain still so fresh in me that surely, I traced the outline of his jaw with my finger, maybe brought the image to my lips. I have looked at it for so many years now, I no longer see it.

At the put-in, on the concrete ramp that leads into the Selway, I watch your six-foot-four frame slide easily into the new pack raft you bought earlier this year. This will be its second trip. The longest in the new boat. You do the same hop and scoot I watched Randy do so many times. First bow, then the body, touches the water, and soon the whole boat is lifted from the rocks, and you are floating. I bring my camera to my eye and find you in the frame. I click and hear the mechanical shutter sound. I click again. And again. I cannot see your face. But I know you are looking at me.

Soon your friends join in their kayaks, and all of you begin to float downstream. You pivot your boat around and wave. I take three more pictures. Zoom in as far as I can to see you, take another, and then climb up the bank to your truck. I told you I would likely hike down the trail along the river for a while. I lied.

Randy had blown kisses. He was across the river from me the last time I saw him. I don't remember now if I waited for him and Jim to put their boats back in the water or turned and left, limping back to the truck. I was recovering from a broken ankle. An accident had on the unfinished steps at our house, when I turned to laugh at something Randy said, caught my foot between the open space between step and riser, and spun around on what once was a very stable joint. It was a week before we were to leave on our honeymoon. I wish I remember what Randy said because it was funny, and I would like the chance to laugh at it again. My ankle was broken. Shattered. There would be surgery and no honeymoon, even though we had rescheduled for a later date after the cast came off. I hobbled away from the river, and I never saw Randy alive again.

Leaning against your truck, I rehearse what I will say when the sheriff meets me at the takeout. Or when I finally get to cell service, and there is a call, maybe it is Joe's wife or your mother. Maybe there will be a crowd gathered at Selway Falls and a coroner's van. I will overhear someone say, "They haven't found the body," or "he is pinned under a log, and it may be a while before we can get the equipment in to get him out," or "They left his body on the trail and the search and rescue guys are hiking in to get it." I tell myself that when I hear these words, I will not believe it is you. It will be someone else they are talking about. When I find out it is you. I will stand very still. After telling the sheriff, "I am his partner." I will do exactly what he and the crowd expect me to do. I don't want my reaction to seem practiced. So as my hands go to my face to cover my mouth in that cliched way, I'll act surprised and in disbelief, but already I will be working out my escape. I will let the tears fall until some brave person approaches me, and then I will ask to see you. Ask where you are.

In my mind, I will be packing up the house, deciding what needs to go. I will be dumping every ounce of liquor from the cabinet. Giving away house plants and turning off the water. I will stay in McCall only as long as your funeral, and the whole time I am there, I will pack. I will pack and pack and throw things away, and I will not answer the phone or the eyes of friends and family who will be asking, *How could this happen to her again?* I will let myself believe I am cursed. I will let this be the excuse as to why I never get into another romantic relationship. And as lookers-on gasp and secretly take pictures of me or us, as they did from Painter's Bridge the day I lay with Randy's body until finally I yelled, "Get the fuck out of here," I will already be in another town, starting a new life, avoiding questions and lying when I don't. I will tell these lies so often and so perfectly that eventually, even I will believe them.

I will not be drunk at your funeral. When people say to me, "Don't worry, you will find someone new," I will not tell them to go to hell. I will not forsake my dogs, sleep in the closet, or throw your mother's china to the floor just to break the goddamned silence you leave me. I will tell my mother and friends that I am used to this. No, they needn't come to stay with me. I always knew this day would come. I will not squander your money. I will not live on a diet of hot dogs and mayonnaise, nor will I take all the Xanax they prescribe me with all the scotch in the house and tell myself it is just to help me sleep.

What I will not have control over are the dreams. Dreams of us together in some bright meadow as we are now most days in the summer. Dreams of you and me on a boat or a train, as I was with Randy for years after he died. Dreams of your anger at me for selling the house, getting rid of your things. I will not be able to say, "My dead husband," as I do now when I talk about Randy. I will have to say, "My first dead husband," or "my latest…" And I will laugh a little afterward, and when people get home to their spouses, they will whisper, "I think she might have gone crazy". I will not be crazy, only drowning in grief, and this will be unfortunate.

I get in the truck and wait to start the motor. I want you to believe that I am going to hike as I said I would. I want you to think that if you were to get out of your boat and touch the trail, you would be touching me. But I want away from the river. I tell myself I need ice. I want a real cup of coffee to make up for the instant you gave me at camp only a couple of hours ago. Just the ice and I will head back with the dogs to the woods where books and notebooks and a fine campsite next to Lake Como or Painted Rocks Lake will hold me. I will back the truck up to the water and stare across it until the sun sets and try to imagine you and Chris and Joe at your own camp fifteen or so miles from where I left you this morning. Your faces are vibrant and lit by your campfire.

Before the coroner drove away Randy's body, I asked to see him. She opened one of the van's two back doors, and I climbed inside. I unzipped the bag very slowly; I did not want to catch Randy's hair, scrape his nose. I cannot remember if his eyes were open or closed—only that they were blue. I remember his brown hair still wet with river water. His lips dry where mine had been. I tried to hug him. I wanted to pull out his hand, to hold it. I think I remember his lips slightly smiling. Or was his mouth open? That night I would make my mind's eye go over every inch of his body again and again. I would memorize it. I would forget the coroner reaching in before rezipping the bag and running her fingers through his hair, saying, "He had such great hair."

Two days pass, and I am at the little convenience store across the bridge that goes over the river at the confluence of the Lochsa and the Selway. I ask the cashier if there have been any reports of drownings. I am thumbing sale shirts on a rack, acting like he must get this question all the time. I tell him my first husband died kayaking, and fear is my companion when my current partner is on the water. He avoids my eyes as I hand him my credit card, and I smile at this, feeling agency—the power I need for what may be to come.

The road along the Selway is not as thin as that we drove along Deep Creek. It would take a lot of high water or some really bad choices to put a truck in the river here. I stop to pull plums from a roadside tree. The air conditioner is all the way up, and still, the dogs pant in the seat behind me.

Despite having the map, I make a wrong turn. It takes me fifteen minutes to find a wide enough place to turn around and make my way to where you said you would meet me. I back the truck up to the river and open the tailgate. The sand is too hot for the dogs' paws, so they jump into the bed and take comfort in the shade and lap greedily at the iced-down water I give them. I watch the river for a helmet, for an empty kayak that might come floating by. Practicing is how I get through.

Friends, when they lose their spouses, ask me how to get through the first night. What I want to say to them is that you don't get through it. Or over it. You get used to it. I tell them the pain will come in waves, and sometimes those waves will be so big that they take you under; other times, it will be a scent or someone walking down the street that you are sure is your beloved, and then catch up to them, and just as you about to tap their shoulder you realize this impossibility and you and the wave recede. No, they are not coming back.

No.

How many things end so finally as they do when the bow of a boat touches the bank of a river after days of riding it's current? One minute you are being carried by unforgiving water, and the next you are rising out of your boat, feet on the same sand as mine. It's hot. So you pull off your black helmet, fill it from the river, and then pour it over your hair and head. It falls to your shoulders, runs the length of your body, then drains back into the Selway. From here, it will travel to the Clearwater, the Columbia, and then all the way to the Pacific.

The Place Between the Stars

The red dot appears and disappears. A memorized pattern. Slide the safety up, the red dot disappears, and the rifle will not fire; down, and the trigger is free. This I learned young. This was part of my raising. Clear and open the chamber before anything else, never point the barrel at something you aren't planning to kill, keep the safety on until you are ready to shoot. The red dot is gone. I have the rifle pointed at a cow elk. The crosshairs jerk around her body, I push the safety back on. She turns her head to look at me. Others are standing with her, more cows. Five, at least. Some behind her. They are all outlined by a sky going blue to gray. Even if I could steady the crosshairs, the bullet could pass through. Caleb waits in the trees, not wanting to scare the small herd. I kneel and then lie prostrate on the frozen ground, but the ridge they walk is too high for a lying down shot. Safety on. I sit and balance the barrel on my knees.

Same position, different animal. A buck. Late October, five years earlier. We had walked the trail to Krassel Knob in the dark before morning following only the red beam of the headlamp. I was warm with a strange sense of safety. The 30.06 over my shoulder, an assumed protection from anything outside the red beam. In the early dawn light, I lay down twice with the rifle pointed at a deer. The first time, a small buck, probably too far away anyhow, spooked at our scent. The wind favored the animal. The second time, I belly crawled for 50 yards toward a small herd of lounging does, certain a young male would be in their midst. Finally, they rose and ran, and there was no buck.

Morning had become late afternoon and we had become louder, hunters turned hikers, cutting our way through a ravine that would take us back to the trail. Caleb was carrying the gun as sometimes he does when we are moving fast, lightening my load. I will always remember the sun on that day. The way it poured into that late October landscape, turning grass golden, gilding the tops of trees rising from the steep hillsides. The sun lay like a tired mother in the bottom of the ravine when a buck stepped into her light. He paused as mule deer are want to do then spooked. Like us, he was moving fast, unwittingly, but filled with other desires. He looked right past us in our slipshod camo. His nose lifted to air, smelling something. The does on the hillside, perhaps. He was stupid with lust and rut.

This one's yours, Caleb whispered. He handed me the gun. I needed to slow my breath. I raised the rifle, closed my left eye. My father's voice told me to inhale, pull the trigger, exhale. Don't blink. I had been lucky two seasons in a row. Clean shots both. Perhaps luck inspired a confidence I relied too heavily upon—maybe I was still stupid with rut as well. I inhaled, slid the safety up. Fired. Missed. Chambered another bullet. Fired. Hit the buck, though I couldn't tell where, and he ran. We held there a moment. I shook my head, *It wasn't a good shot.* When I squeezed the trigger, I had closed my eyes. Something I did not do when, years earlier, I shot the buck my late husband, Randy, and I had watched grow from a gangly spike. We had a pact; we wouldn't kill anything that grazed in our 60 acres that were once planted in alfalfa and still gave us volunteer graze. Our horses spent spring mornings in it, fall afternoons, too. It fed them and a small herd of whitetail. Sometimes, antelope.

I mounted the head of the buck I promised not to kill and called it Boom. *Boom* and it was dead, I told my friend as we dressed it out and hung it in his barn. Later, along with his wife, we three would process the deer we each shot. Warm up the woodstove and make sausage, wrap steaks, stand on woodchips while saws and grinders worked. Dressed, processed, boom. The words we use to help distance the pain of killing. *He drowned*, I would tell people when they asked how Randy died. I no longer called it an accident, nor said *I lost him when I was just 30*, he had not simply *passed away*. *He died doing what he loved*, someone said to me at his funeral. *He loved living*, I replied. Boom. I can't imagine an animal giving itself to me; I believe everything living, save for the deeply tormented, wants to continue to live. It's what we know. The cow elk on the hillside sniffed the air, nosing a smell she wasn't sure of. She wasn't poised to run. None of them were. They were merely grazing in what was left of the late December sun. *Will the elk be pregnant?* I had asked Caleb. *Yes*, he said. When I asked how big the fetus would be, he said, *You won't be able to tell.*

We had to put chains on the truck to make it up the grade. I had drawn a late cow elk hunt tag. The region was steep and mostly inaccessible, likely the reason the tags were available. We had hunted the gulch across the ravine the weekend before but went home empty. This was my last chance. Christmas was coming. We would soon leave to visit my mother in Colorado. We needed time to hang and process the animal. And weather was coming. Snow. NOAA issued a Winter Storm Warning. If I was going to shoot an elk, it had to be before sundown. The grade was a hill by Idaho standards, but like most places we hunted, it was precipitous. Even with the chains, we occasionally slid. I looked out my window and could see no road, no ledge. Just down. If we went off here, the truck would roll. Wheels, cab, wheels, cab. It wouldn't stop until it reached the road. The dogs were in the backseat, sleeping. Their trust in us is so complete. The rifle lay in its hard black case beside them, as if it was a third dog, sleeping, trusting. I remember a story my father told me about his father and a small dog they had. "Take it hunting and don't bring it back," my grandfather said to his son. "What did you do?" I asked. I remember him saying he tried to pretend it was a rabbit. He was not one to dress up the truth. The morning Mark Cada killed himself, Dad took me downstairs and handed me a bullet. "Mark put this through his head." The bullet was as long as one of my fingers. Heavy. I couldn't picture what Mark's father found when he found Mark on the hillside above their house, but forty years later, when a poet, a classmate, sat on a bench in the university's arboretum and pulled his trigger, I saw it perfectly. *There is a hole where they dug up the blood*, a friend whispered as we walked. I hoped some of his blood would find the roots of the tree he sat beneath. To keep some of him living with the poems he left behind.

I think of the last breath my husband released into the Clarks Fork River on the afternoon he drowned. I wonder if another being inhaled it. Maybe some of him went on. We poured his ashes into a different river in the hours after his memorial. I had picked the ashes up from the funeral home where I had last seen him, or rather, his body. The smear of white spit was still crusted on his lips where I had pressed my own and tasted nothing but river water. Someone had led me into a darkened room to be alone with his body a final time. I only remember the spit and the dark and the husband of one of Randy's sisters taking me out with a firm hand on my arm. I had ridden to the funeral home with his family. Closed in the car his mother said, "You lied about being married." It was two days before his funeral. "We were married," I told her. Just as I had told her the night she and his father drove to the mortuary across the state line, to see for themselves, that he was dead. We were in a gas station. She said there had been a mistake, the coroner had listed me as his spouse. That she corrected it. "It was no mistake," I told her. Reaching for a drink I wouldn't finish, I told her we were married. "Joint taxes," I muttered. The car was silent after I spoke. At Randy's funeral, seconds after the colonel placed a flag in my hands and saluted me, she tore the flag from my arms, where I'd pressed it to my chest. "He was mine," she said so loud she startled the priest.

The 30.06 in the backseat was Randy's. I bought it at a pawn shop. A Christmas gift. I killed Boom with it after Randy died. I was packing up the house because I couldn't make the mortgage payments—even if I could, the house was not in my name. Just a week before he died, Randy had removed the pay on death insurance. Nothing was in my name. He had no will. That's when lawyers got involved. It was only two weeks after his funeral. His parents made demands, called a meeting between our lawyers. Everyone showed up but his mom and dad. Driving home, my best friend Melissa at the wheel, we watched as a hawk lifted from the ground, a black snake in its mouth. "You will win this," she said. And as she did, the hawk dropped the snake which writhed in the air until it hit the ground in a place neither of us saw. I had found a dead hawk on our deck the week before Randy died. *It's a chicken*, he tried to convince me, but I know hawks. Even then they meant something. Omens, harbingers. The knowing began with a young hawk I found in a blizzard and warmed back to health in my bathroom. Its enlivening cry filled every corner of my house. For months after it flew from my door, I would see it sitting in the pine near my house. Randy dug a hole and we buried the hawk outside the fence we'd strung for our four dogs.

Rusty was the newest of the four. He came from a family who asked us to take care of him while they traveled. They never came back for him. In a sympathy card the wife wrote, *We are so sorry for your loss. If Rusty is too much, we will come get him.* Boom. The words we use to distance us from pain. In a photo taken years later, Rusty sits beside my dad under the black walnut tree in the front yard of my childhood home. Dad, in his ridiculous gardening hat, balances a huge squash with one hand and has his other arm around the big red dog. He was just starting to forget things when he and Mom drove from Colorado to my house in Montana to help me move. Dad spent mornings spreading the gravel

I'd had delivered as a Father's Day gift to Randy from the dogs. Mom packed dishes in old newspapers. I sorted through Randy's military records and photographs. We are a family who works as we grieve.

The buck I'd shot on the late October afternoon was gone. We were tracking it by drops of blood barely visible on the tips of brown grass. Every few yards, a spattering marked a place where the animal paused as the blood left his body. The buck had climbed out of the ravine, crossed the trail we sought, and was headed for a deeper drainage. We tied flagging in places where we found blood. It began to snow. I was angry at Caleb. I'd felt pressured. He'd whispered excitedly, *this one is yours. You got this. Careful. Breathe. Aim for the heart.* We had not known each other long. Only hunted together for two seasons. Caleb had given up hunting before we met; it was me who talked him back into it. Handed him the rifle my father gave me, the .308 with a stock in which my dad inlaid twelve unique types of wood to make a diamond pattern. It was the only gun my parents had for the first decade of their marriage. The means of survival in 1950s Montana when survival, for them, was hard to come by. Caleb and I moved slowly through the long grass, nearly invisible to one another in our camo and the darkening forest. Still quiet. Still hunting. When finally, we saw one another he whispered about the coming darkness, the snow beginning to fall. *You should go get the dogs and bring them back here.* I nodded. He would keep tracking, and as I turned, he added *bring the meat pack.* All the way back to the truck I replayed the shot. The crack of the rifle. The startled face of the buck. Rechambering. Again. And the buck running on three legs. Shame carried me down the darkening trail. I pulled the trigger in haste. I was in love. I wanted to impress Caleb. I wanted to make him proud the same way I wanted to make my father proud by shooting the robins out of our backyard cherry trees. After my father praised my aim and the cherries saved for winter pies, I would find the bodies of the robins, stroke their smooth chests, and whisper, *I'm sorry.* I could not camouflage my shame. I wore it into my adult life and again on that autumn trail. What kind of person will kill what they love to earn love? What exactly was I aiming at when I finally pulled the trigger?

Buster, the blue heeler Randy had when I met him, is buried in a grove of aspen in Colorado. He should be at my childhood home with Rusty, Maggie, all my childhood dogs, and every childhood pet, from fish to rat that I ever called mine. When I buried Buster, I was dating my horseshoer. He was the kind of man you date when your father is dying and you don't want to face the fact that your father is dying. The kind that talks incessantly about his ex and how much he still loves her, the kind that answers a knock on his door, right after you've had sex, to take a Valentine's gift from that same ex. I was visiting with Buster and Katie. Maggie and Rusty now lived with my mom and dad. I could find no rental that would take four dogs and two horses, my dowry for widowhood, after selling the house Randy and I finished together, the house and acreage I could no longer afford. Randy's mother wanted me to give the horses to a woman in Tennessee. *It would mean so much to her to have something of Randy's,* his mother said, his mother who, following Randy's funeral, demanded back every Christmas gift his family ever gave us. The woman who hung her son's uniform in her living room. Who I did not fight for the life insurance or the flag she had pulled from my hands after the officer placed it there saying, *He made his country proud.* The woman who demanded control of our finances and that Randy's dad be our personal representative. But who I would not give control of our checking account, home, vehicles, or pets to. *It would mean so much to his dad to be in charge of Randy's finances,* she said on the phone. His dad, however, said little, except that I was nice to him. His mother told the lawyers that I was a certain type of woman, this she knew by my belly button piercing and the thong underwear I wore. How she knew about either, I do not know. My lawyer explained that our CPA would testify that Randy understood filing joint taxes meant legal marriage in the state of Montana. *Not in God's eyes*, the former Sunday school teacher said. *You can ask God and Randy when you see them,* I said in a fit of anger. "There are things that happen in a couple's bed that a man doesn't tell his mother," their family lawyer told her. The horseshoer eventually married his ex. *It's best if I don't ever talk to you again,* he said over the phone. I replaced him with a biologist who stopped to see two ex-girlfriends of his own on the way to see me in Taos, where I was trying to escape the pain of my father's death that spring.

Chains rattling, we inched our way up the mountainside to the top where Caleb thought it best to park, knowing even chains might not get us out if we went further. Two men walked out of the trees carrying rifles, Caleb rolled his window down. They said they were hunting wolves and heading home empty-handed. *Take that dog hunting and don't bring it back.* I looked away and listened to the window as it rolled up, snugging glass into weatherstripping. We left the dogs in the truck with a bowl of water and a promise that we would be right back. Randy had blown me kisses from across the river that had drowned him. I was going to the little market near the bridge; I'd be right back, meet him and his friend at the takeout. I was handing money to the clerk when a woman rushed in and said someone had fallen into the river. I assured them both that my husband, the former medevac pilot, would find them. I called him *my husband.* I had been engaged before but never married. I was 32, still trying the word *husband* on, liking it, especially on the day when, Christmas shopping, my best friend said to the clerk, "We have to stop or our husbands are not going to let us go shopping together anymore." I felt a belonging I hadn't known. I felt wanted.

Cisco, a dog Caleb and I adopted, worries when his collar is removed, puts his tail between his legs, lays his ears flat. "You're *our* dog," I said to him over and over the day we brought him home. "*Ours,*" as I put the collar on, shiny and silver. He never seems to mind waiting in the truck. His trust is the same as the trust we have that those we love will always return. Sometimes we tiptoe to the glass and look in at them innocently curled together, and then we unlock the door and scatter them with joy.

The dogs were at the door of the camper when I pulled up to it, in the coming dark on the South Fork. They were still wagging and greeting when I returned to the trail we would walk to find Caleb, and I hoped, the wounded buck. Ten minutes in, I heard the report of the rifle and knew the hunt was over. The dogs stopped and looked at me, the sound too distant to frighten them entirely, but close enough for worry, then we three began to run toward it. I found Caleb on the trail, eyes and face not belying his deed. We stood silent, facing one another, not blinking back the tears or trying to explain them. The buck had laid down above a small creek and Caleb had taken a clean, fatal shot. Now the 30.06 was silent, the chamber open, rendering it impotent. Randy's Christmas present from me a decade before. He had not lived to use it. On a late September afternoon, packing the house we'd shared, packing what was left of the us we had become, I took the gun from its rack on the wall, walked outside in my socks, inhaled, slid the safety down, exhaled, and shot Boom. I fired again, thinking he had not fallen, and the bullet puffed dirt where red chert arrowheads could still be found. I used to think that when I finally did find one of those arrowheads, it would mean I was home. Only two months earlier had I found one in the yard we'd made for our dogs. It was already in a moving box, packed away with an old ashtray and a dime from 1910. My neighbor and her husband had been watching the buck through their binoculars from a butte that belonged to neither of us. They walked out of the trees and knelt next to me. "We got the whole thing on video," the wife said, exuberant. I recalled the people with their cameras standing on the bridge as I lay with Randy's body on the shore of the river he'd just been pulled from. I yelled obscenities at those people with words and hand gestures. "Delete it. Now." I told my neighbor.

After Caleb delivered the fatal shot, the buck's body rolled from where it lay on the hillside down to the creek bank. We cleaned it there. Carefully washing the blood off the warm flesh. *I'm sorry. I'm so sorry.* I said, stroking his fur. "I'm sorry," Caleb said later. "I should have stayed quiet, let you take the shot when you wanted to." Words distance us from pain. Boom. I have not shot a deer since.

Randy's mother blamed me for his death. She said I encouraged his kayaking. True, I had bought him the boat that he had died in. He had bought the forty-year-old scotch that I drank to chase down the Xanax a doctor prescribed me a month after he died. I thought it might kill me. I hoped it would. Our house was so far from everyone. My parents had gone home, though my mother called every night. "Pretend he is still alive," said the mother of the son who killed himself in their backyard. I shot robins from trees as if I enjoyed it and then gave each a silent funeral as Dad sat at the table reading the afternoon paper and Mom cooked supper. Their solitary sacrifices were wrought in the name of love. I let the farrier convince me that Buster, at 20, needed to be *put to sleep*. Words distance us from pain. I convinced myself that the wildlife biologist with a history of anger would never get angry with me again. I shook my head at the man who was with Randy on the river when he died after he said, "You'll meet someone you love more than you ever loved Randy." I let Randy's mother take the flag from my hands and said nothing that night when we poured his ashes into the river, and she told her friend's daughter she had always hoped the two of them would get married. All of this, as if I was not standing right there, as if I was not trying to live. *Ask him when you get there*, I told her again, years after his death, her still questioning his love for me when she called each holiday to remind me that she missed him, making sure I still did, until finally I begged her to stop calling and pretending it was about Randy. Years later I came across a 50th anniversary announcement Randy's parents placed in the local paper which only mentioned two daughters, never a son. The bullet my father handed me in our basement that morning in January was cold in my 8-year-old hand. My father offered no admonishment and gave no explanation; he just sat in his chair looking at me holding the bullet. I pretend to know what he is thinking. The snake falls from the hawk's grip and lands out of sight.

The red dot goes away as I slide the lever up. I slide it back down. Caleb walks out from the trees. I balance the barrel on my knees and aim it at the cow elk. The crosshairs circle a smaller patch of body. The shoulder. Inhale. Exhale. I slide the safety up. My cheek is still pressed to the stock of the gun. My father's 30-30 now in the safe with guns we may never shoot again. My friend's father restored the inlaid stock after it had gotten wet and the glaze turned milky as cataracted eyes. "Your father was a craftsman," he said, handing me the gun. A dozen unique pieces of wood made diamond shapes in the stock. My father, the craftsman, milky with Alzheimer's, unholstered his finger, pointed it at me, "You. Get out." The red dot disappears. The dot of blood on the breast of the last robin I shot. The BB gun in the safe. The cow elk on the ridge, the others moving away from her now. *She was giving herself to you*, my friend said. My Katie dog on the floor of our cabin. Caleb and I holding her as she struggled against the poison that was trying to stop her heart. "I've never seen a dog try so hard to keep living," the vet said, "she didn't want to leave you." The receipt for this read, *Euthanasia. She didn't want to leave you.* Words distance us from pain. Caleb carried her body, wrapped in a wool blanket, to a hole he had dug in our woods. "You'll find someone you love even more," said the man who last saw Randy alive. Katie's collar hangs beside my bed. Carhartt lies beside her grave. The crosshairs draw a smaller pattern on the elk's shoulder. The red dot reappears.

Eight years after Randy died, I fell in love. "You've unlocked every gate," Caleb tells me on the phone. Words distance us, even from love. I drive from my childhood home where so many of my loves are buried, to a town in southeastern Idaho where we will meet for the first time since meeting online. The parking lot of a restaurant where we would not eat dinner, we would not eat at all that first night. Caleb holds a Mason jar full of wildflowers, "Just like the John Denver song," he would tell his mom, who never, like Randy's mother, tells me that I have arranged our kitchen wrong or that I am wasteful with dryer lint that should be placed outside for chickadees to use in their nests. "I know they are talking about me," his mother says to Randy and me when we come for supper one Sunday. "Listen, they say my name over and over, chick a *-dee-dee-dee.*" I wonder if I would recognize my dead husband's voice. My dad, however, sings to me from a cassette recorded in 1976 for my grandparents. I was four and had gotten a piano for Christmas. Caleb and I call the lodgepole nearest our house, Winston, after George Winston, the pianist whose music fills our home. Chickadees sit in Winston's limbs waiting for the larger birds to leave the feeder. I can't stop hearing Randy's mother, so I learn to love robin song and the tapping of nuthatch as they seek bugs in the wood of our home. Sometimes we sit together on the couch, Caleb and me and two dogs, and stare into the trees.

"I like sitting beside you," Caleb says. And Katie lies in the earth beyond the house, and Carhartt suffers vestibular attacks and, for a short while, cannot walk without falling over, and we know that 16 years is a long time for a dog, but she makes lap after lap around the house as if guarding the love we keep inside.

The meat from Boom rots when the freezer that holds it quits. Boom's head falls off the wall in a house I rent and one of the antlers comes off. I think I should bury it, but I don't. What does one do with something they have paid to make lifelike but that nevertheless aims to prove its death? Both antler and head are in storage, along with many of my other belongings, stashed there when I said yes to Caleb when after three dates he asked if I wanted to move in with him. One day, I tell myself, I will clean out that storage unit, stop paying rent to store memories, donate Randy's clothes and cowboy hats, bury Boom's head in my mother's backyard alongside all the other animals I loved. What else is one to do with the things we hold onto in a fierce effort to keep them alive? I believe the elk wanted to live. Randy once said he would die before he reached 35. "I thought he would climb up on the rock," the last man to see Randy alive would say. Randy blew me kisses the last time I saw him alive. The elk is standing alone on the ridgeline.

I was alone in the big house on Blanchard Butte Road for two days after Randy died. My uterus emptied what Randy and I had made only a few weeks before. This was not the first time. I remember him crying months earlier, leaving for a work trip and leaving me with blood and a bag filled with aftercare. I would be ok, I told him as I was leaving the clinic. That night I passed out in a hotel room because I lacked the strength to make the 30-minute drive home. *About how big*, I asked Caleb, who I know I love because he has the answers to the same questions my father would have the answers to. Questions about wildlife and trails and mountains and weather. How to stay alive for weeks in the wild. *Maybe the size of a pea.* Caleb tells me and leaves me to decide if I still want to hunt. My father, thinking of his father, and the dog he shot, *I pretended it was a rabbit.* Caleb taking the meat pack off his back, guiding the barrel of my rifle through its crossbars, the crosshairs steadying. The elk stands alone on the ridgeline. The sky behind her is turning steel gray, gun-barrel gray. Behind me, the jagged teeth of the Seven Devils range bite into the sky.

The first thing we saw as we started down the trail that early winter morning were fresh wolf tracks centered in the boot prints of the unsuccessful hunters. We were walking through a stand of bare aspen. The trail was unlike most Idaho trails we'd walked. It was flat and descending. When we cleared the trees, we could see over the river some five hundred feet below to a ridge we had hunted the week before. That had been a nasty climb. Steep. Snowy. We had glassed elk in the trees above the knob, and as I belly crawled the final distance, I was louder than I could have been. I hoped they heard me. It was at least four miles back to the truck. It would take three trips to pack the animal out. I didn't want to climb that hill again, not once, certainly not twice. Not to slide down the slope, slippery with the season. I hadn't cried because I wounded the deer those years before on the South Fork; I cried because Caleb was crying. Our instinct is to survive. Wounded, I have run. The morning my father died, I was dress shopping. My sister texted me: *He is gone.* I was in the dressing room with the dress I would buy and wear to his funeral. I have forgotten now what that dress looked like. I cannot remember what else is in the storage unit, Randy's voice, or if he said it was 35 he would not live beyond, or 40. This year I turned 50 and bled for two weeks straight. I thought I would be past this by now.

Caleb wonders when I will stop writing about my dad and Randy. He says, "I am not like Randy or your dad," when I suggest we remodel the house. He has killed two deer with the rifle I bought for Randy, not including the buck I attempted to kill. *I like sitting beside you.* I tell him that I am ready to sell the armoire that was Randy's, one of the few pieces of furniture I brought with me. The widow's dowry. *Pretend he is still alive.* The mirror on the front of the armoire is old and distorts the way I see myself. The backing is coming off, and there are places where I can see through, to the inside, as if it were plain glass, which all mirrors, finally stripped of their silvering, are.

We had convinced ourselves we would see no elk that day. They'd be hunkered down in the trees, preparing for the coming storm. And there had been the wolf hunters, and there were the wolves, so Caleb slung the unloaded rifle over his shoulder, and we walked as if it were a summer trail. But there were elk. And we'd not have known if we had not stopped for lunch and started glassing the slope below us and seen the bulls. Carefree, their dangerous season over, one pair lying butt to butt, arrogant in their safety. More were scattered on the ridges and precipices below them. The snow had not yet started and the trail went farther and we are those people who always want to see what is around the next corner, so we walked on. And around the corner is where we found ourselves, unprepared for the cow elk. Caleb chambered a bullet, handing me the gun, saying nothing as I walked, then crawled down the trail. The elk still. Alone now, I take a shallow breath and press my cheek to the stock, moving my eye close to the scope, a scope I looked through years ago to kill a coyote who was caught in a trap and whose leg was shattered. I had a pistol, but I needed distance. That afternoon it was the hood of my pickup that balanced the rifle. I couldn't bear the suffering. The cries. The way the animal leapt over and over again as if by some miracle it would finally be free. We try so hard to get away from pain. The report of the 30.06 is so loud. I wanted it to be louder. I screamed when Buster took his last breath, I screamed again when I felt Katie's body go limp. The rifle's report would echo across the ridgeline and be gone. Mine would echo throughout time and memory. The sound is a result of a small combustion, a release. *Boom. Ok,* I said when the EMT said Randy was dead. *Ok,* I texted my sister.

When Caleb tells the story of the cow elk the following spring to our friends who have come to visit, he starts crying. *I could tell she was scared,* he said. *She kept pushing the safety on and off. Her hands were shaking.* We were sharing supper. Elk steaks. I have come to like telling the story of the meat we serve. The meat we have killed. I sometimes tell the story of Caleb standing at the sink with a three-toed salamander in his hands. An exterminator had been called to kill the ants that had burrowed into our home. The poison had found all the living things, including the salamander that lived beneath the plywood that protects our windows from shattering under the pressure of the snow when it gets deep. He was holding the creature so gently in his big hands, the same way he holds the story of the cow elk. The stream of water from the faucet was warm and he was running a fingertip up and down the length of its body, which he then returned to safety. I slide the safety off. The pack Caleb used to carry the quarters of the buck out of the South Fork was before me. I guide the barrel through the crossbars, and I feel a weight lifted. I press the stock against my shoulder. My cheekbone against the stock. My left eye closed, my right one seeks that place on the animal that will promise instant death. Above the shoulder, below the neck. I aim for the heart.

When I was young, I often spent summer nights sleeping beside my dog on the grass in our backyard. One of those nights, when I was eight or ten, I heard our screen door open and saw my dad step out. He walked through the night and then laid down beside me. I was never in trouble for sneaking outside to sleep. This of himself, my father saw in me. We lay side-by-side and stared at the stars. The planets. The Milky Way. I remember the sky as a brighter blue than it should have been and my father saying that if I wanted to see the stars clearly, I would have to stare at the darkness between them. The heart lies in the place between the neck and the shoulder. The crosshairs no longer wander. The safety is on. And then it is not.

It is the moments between that have changed me. Pulling the trigger never hurts as much as finding the animal lying dead on the slope, body pressed against one of only two Douglas firs on the ridgeline. Darkening the red dot when I feel Caleb sit behind me on the trail, his chest to my back, his heart pressed to my spine. He wrapped his arms around me and closed the space between his body and mine. I never know when the right time comes. I only know that something comes over me, perhaps an ancient need for survival, a space when the tightening of my finger pulls the trigger less than one-sixteenth of an inch. I keep my right eye open, my right thumb slides the safety back off. It all happens in less than three seconds.

And the dogs will be waiting in the truck, and the storm will come, and it will take two trips of four miles, and I will watch as Caleb heaves the pack that carried two of the elk quarters onto his back, and I will try to relieve his weight by placing my trekking poles under his pack, my only weight being the meat from the ribs, the liver, the heart. This alone, is all that I can carry.

We will make the last trip to the truck just as the snow begins to fall and we will drive down the steep road following our headlights, putting our trust in that singular vision, knowing that to leave the road could mean safety or certain death. Our tracks will be covered by morning. On the hillside, now indelible in my memory, we have left the carriage of the cow elk. We have left some scraps for the others who must survive a winter that will be as challenging as any we have known. Eventually, her bones, like the bones of everything I have or will ever love, will return to the earth. Though it will take time. And I will return to them in summer, sit in the shade of the tall pine, stare out at the Seven Devils still cloaked in winter snow, and trace the long surface of a rib bone and reach once again, for the heart.

Summit Lake

It finally cooled off enough last night so that this morning I had to put on a robe. Cool enough to close the windows upon waking. Cool enough that Caleb and I could tease each other about starting a fire in the wood stove. A fire, now, in late August.

Yesterday we left after lunch to get a load of firewood. An autumn task, yet it still felt like summer to me. The light, the air, they hadn't seemed to make the subtle shift from the intensity of summer to the ease of autumn. Flowers still bloom along our driveway, a non-native variety of yellow daisies and native gray pussytoes. The fireweed flowers have only started to open. But in the high country where Caleb fell the Doug-fir, the tall cone-shaped fireweed has bloomed its fuchsia flowers to the tip, and seeds of white fuzz, looking not unlike smoke, hang on to pink stems. The old timers would say this is a sign that snow can fall any day now.

We have seen snow early here. As early as Labor Day back in 2015. That year, we hiked in the blustery gray of a near blizzard to Duck Lake. But, if I remember correctly, what snow did fall melted the next morning and the season opened into a long, beautiful Indian Summer. I have often wondered what that means, Indian Summer, so this morning I looked it up. Although its exact origin is unknown, the internet suggests that is likely so-called because of descriptions given to Native people by white settlers about the time after hot summer when the land is cooling, but still warm, before the heavy storms, or one online source suggested, it was based on a time in autumn when tribes hunted.

This definition seems loose and contrived. Native people are known to have hunted year-round without regard to season. No matter the definition, I like the sound of it. Indian Summer. It sounds hopeful. A month or a few weeks when we still have time, a season not over yet, an autumn not begun. And there is something in the gentleness of the season that reminds me of love and kindness, though I cannot quite put my finger on it. Settling in. Into home. Into one another. A time of gathering food, and family. Of stowing summer memories. A recounting season.

Oh, and the colors of an Indian Summer! Please do not spare me those! Crimson, amber, rust, corn, honey, gold—how many shades of yellow and orange? A death song in technicolor. Colors the notes a cello might make when its strings are stroked in a still Ponderosa forest and held in the overstory for next season's birds to inhale. Those colors, that sound, make a quilt of humus that I could blanket myself in all winter. A quilt I have spent the summer sleeping upon. I lay my head down over and over upon the tender earth of these Salmon River Mountains. I have come to know the sound of them, the heartbeat of granite, and the dreams of trees rooted here for hundreds of years.

Today marks eight years I have lived in West Central Idaho. Here, at more than a mile high. Here among the pine that I greet morning after morning, that I have given names to, proper names, as calling them Douglas-fir or Lodgepole pine was somehow demeaning to a tree most likely here before Latin names, before English. When I can remember the words, I talk to them in nimipuutímt, but that is not my language either. So, most of the time we communicate with silence.

I try to recall my first look out of these tall windows that make up the front of this cabin, a look into the stalwart trees that have held snow fifty feet above us for months at a time, shaded us from ninety-degree days, that protect the grave of my Katie dog, and give home or modest perch to osprey, robin, nuthatch, evening grosbeak, tanager, ravens—all the birds we anticipate spring after spring. Still, I cannot recollect that first moment, only the joy of the first morning when I woke to the smell of damp pine needles on a late summer breeze. A morning not unlike this one.

And not unlike that first morning, we have decided to go for a hike. A lake we have never been to. Summit Lake. Another untrail. All summer we have been hiking trailless ridgelines. Bushwhacking through ravines or slipping on pine needles to rarely visited lakes and seldom hiked mountain tops. Caleb, my partner for these last eight years, and my reason for coming to central Idaho opens the map, picks a lake, a peak, often unnamed, and the dogs and I willingly follow. Our hike to Summit Lake will likely be our last of the season. There is more wood to collect. Jobs and weather call us inside. And when hunting, the dynamic will change. Our reason for being in the forest will shift. We will be quieter selves. We will have rifles, and they will create a wholly different presence in the woods. One perhaps even we enjoy a little less. But for now, we are still summer reckless, free of that responsibility.

Summit Lake is near Secesh Summit west of McCall, south of Burgdorf hot springs. A glance at the map proves that it is not far from the road where we will park, but it is challenging. Fallen trees, thick brush, steep grade, fire scar. We have hiked in this area of the Payette National Forest before, eight years ago, in the autumn when I first moved here. Before the trees in our backyard had their names. Before I slept with my head on this range.

Eight years ago, we hiked a loop along Diamond Ridge and came down along the same slope we will take today to Summit Lake. For years after, we would drive by the trailhead, and I would say that I would like to go back to the meadow we encountered on that first hike. I can still picture it. No, that is not right. I still feel it. Perhaps I can best describe it as the way I imagine one to feel when one finds God. Or maybe it is more like the feeling of great relief. Being granted amnesty. Or perhaps it is that on that day I knew joy as a feeling and not just a word. And I want to say love, but it is not quite that, and yet, it is that too. What I can say is that when I first walked into it, into the meadow, it was lush, verdant, and even in late August, a translucent stream lulled its way over smooth rock, through quaking aspen, around bright purple monkey flowers almost silently. I crept to its edge and lay down in the grass, cool and soft, and smiled at the blue wing of sky that glided through hundred-foot-tall pine—it was joy and it was more than joy, love, and more than love. Christians might use the word Heaven. For me, it was more like a homecoming, but to a place I had never been.

Since then, I have come into a hundred such meadows, each as beautiful as the first and each with the same feeling of welcome.

I look across a drainage to a pocket where I think that first meadow is and for a moment want to tug the sleeve of my companion and ask that we change course. But I turn toward a new destination. There are no meadows on the way to Summit Lake. In fact, it seems almost as if the terrain around the lake is trying to keep us out. Even the first steps from the truck are steep, slick with loose earth. From there, we work our way back and forth along the slope, making our own switchbacks, climbing over fallen trees, over and over the natural history of this place, the years of Native voices, the smell of fires, the droughts, the lightning, the song of birds now gone from this hillside, all held tight in the rings of lodgepole and larch trees. Some I can simply swing my leg over, or step on and over. Others require pulling my five-foot-ten frame up, belly first, and then swinging my body over and sliding off the other side. At times, I rest on the still assuredness of their girth. I place my cheek where only hawks and raindrops have been.

The dogs revel in the cooler air. Carhartt, the elder, perks her ears for the sound of squirrels busy in their preparations, for the chirp of a chipmunk. As soon as she hears that high-pitched bark, her tan, and white body is ageless, jumping trees, running through the turning leaf of the huckleberry. She still has the energy of a young dog. And that wonderful disregard. Caleb will whistle her back, but with age has come a certain amount of impunity. She knows the consequences for not turning back immediately are slight, if they exist at all. Cisco, younger by at least seven years and equally interested in squirrels, returns immediately. His pants audible and his tail thumping against our legs, as if to make certain we know who the good dog is.

This afternoon I let them get ahead of me as we move through a sparse stand of lodgepole pine. I am taking my time. Looking closely and slowly around the woods. Memorizing. The pack on my back is light, and instead of my standard shorts and tank top, I am in long pants and a sweatshirt. Even though I am damp from the work of walking this land, the wind which has been gusting all morning, is cold enough to demand sleeves, protection, and though I was longing for one more day of sun on my arms, bare legs wading through creeks, I comply. If nothing else, I am obedient to the seasons.

It is almost noon. The cant of light through the trees becomes friendly. I pause with the feeling of something familiar. This is not the pressing sun of days before, but more like an old friend coming in the backdoor to visit, sitting easily at the kitchen table. This contented light finds its way to the tiny leaves of the red whortleberry bush and warms its tiny berries thereon. I kneel to the few that are left and place them on my tongue. If fall has a taste in the Salmon River Mountains, it is the acerbic and piquant sweet and sour of the whortleberry and its cousin, the huckleberry. How something so small can fill the mouth with so much anticipation and flavor remains a wonderful mystery that I continue to investigate berry after berry, season after season. No wonder bears will sit among these patches and gorge themselves before, or perhaps as a dessert to, the slugs and ants they forage under the rocks and claw from tree stumps as they prepare for the ensuing winter.

A sudden breeze moves my thoughts from the bear, from the berries to something older. I look up, sniff the wind. The air is bringing with it a smell of elk musk. And a chill from somewhere farther north. And something else, something opposite of the meadow, yet related, a feeling of nostalgia perhaps. And a middle-aged mountain girl's sentimentality for a season. I watch several long leaves of browning red shudder and fall from the alder. The bear grass, which seemed only last week to offer smooth, soft, white gifts of ambrosial flower, is brown and rough and rattles with the wind. My shoulders relax and I smile. Over forty years of mountain living have taught me to recognize this. This is the beginning of autumn.

We decided rather than going to Diamond Point and circling down to the lake, we would take the more direct route across the smaller ridges that separate us. We come first to an intermittent stream, dry now with no more snow melt to fill it, then to a spring. The dogs are grateful. Carhartt, as usual, does not pause, but walks right into the water and lies down, drinking the whole while. I think back to a years ago hike to a place called Hard Butte, a simple stream that I can no better describe than the meadow. The water was so clear that when Carhartt lay down in it, I could not tell where the air ended and water began, save for her hair being lifted by the latter. I drank deep from that Hard Butte spring and, like the meadow at Diamond Ridge, I promised to return. But we haven't yet. And in the interim I have knelt and drank from countless streams and springs, some with water coming straight from the granite mountain.

We reach the lake only after stumbling and slipping down the steep slope that held it. The water, like many of these mountain lakes, is a blue that defies the palette. Clear, but still blue. Azure. Turquoise. I reach my hand in to feel it, tempted to swim one last time in this wilderness immersion font, but then I remember the wind, and I know that drying off won't be as comfortable as it was only a couple of weeks ago when we came out of a lake in the Frank Church Wilderness and laid our naked bodies down upon white granite and in moments were dry and warm.

Caleb begins assembling his fishing pole as the dogs and I find a place to sit in the grass and watch. He brings the lengths together and carefully threads the filament through the guides. He then reaches into his pack for his box of lures, finds something silver and red, threads the line through the smallest hole, and then wraps once, twice, again, again, to form a knot strong enough to hold a fish, should he catch one.

What lives in these waters interests us both. Me, from a somewhat poetic and childish interest; in him it is the scientist that is curious. Caleb is a fisheries biologist for the Payette National Forest. He keeps notes about fish, or the lack of them, for each lake we visit. We have learned that this lake had historically been stocked with brook trout. If there are still fish in this lake, it is because they found a way to survive, a small channel up which to spawn, and a depth they could reach to survive the winter freeze that, at this elevation, may last as long as eight months. There is a tug on the line before he even starts reeling the lure. The fish he catches are small, *snaky* he calls them. Overpopulated, but successful. We watch a male cruise the shoreline. This is his spawning season; his lower belly and dorsal fins reflect the bright red of Oregon grape leaves that surround the lake.

We walk unhurriedly around the shore to the other side. Along the way we spot massive piles of bear scat and are excited about the sow or boar who must live here, who is also feeling the tug of the season, looking carefully for a den in which to hibernate. Six feet up on a spruce trunk someone has attached a wooden sign with Summit Lake carved into it. I ask Caleb if he thinks this is the work of the Forest Service and he shakes his head. Sometimes it is just the way people try to love a place. A dedication. I trace the letters with my finger knowing that this person and I would understand each other, as each of us tries to honor a place with words that seemingly always fall short.

We find a place to sit and eat our lunch and begin the motion of nostalgia. We are listing all the places that we have visited this year. French Lakes, Little French Creek, Williams Peak, Big Creek, Nichol Mountain, Bridal Veil Falls, Coffee Cup Lake, Grassy Twin… we keep listing and talking about the hikes that had no names, the lakes that had no names, how satisfied we were with the way we had spent our summer. We recall the different hikes in a way that one might talk about family, about glory years. "Do you remember the way it felt to open your eyes when swimming in…." and "The view from Big Creek Point…." and "…when we found the old sheep trail…" and "that yellow columbine next to the unnamed stream on the Fall Creek trail. That columbine was incredibly yellow and the first we had seen all season…" and "when we broke out of the brush from walking the old logging road and found ourselves atop that peak all covered in yellow balsamroot arrowleaf and you started crying because of the beauty." "Yes, I remember…"

Carhartt is lying in a shallow hole she has dug for herself in a clearing by a Labrador tea bush, and Cisco is intensely watching black ants as they crawl onto his black and tan and white fur, then picking them up carefully with his front teeth, and swallowing them whole. We go with our recollecting for a while until Caleb finally says aloud what we both know, "This is likely our last hike of the summer. Last hike for hiking's sake." And we grow quiet. The wind through the tops of burned trees once startled a friend visiting from California in early autumn. *Are those wolves?* she asked me. *No.* I reassured her. *Those are pine ghosts singing for snow.* The four of us rise and begin our descent. As we leave Summit Lake behind, the wind and pines make a song that fills the valley, the lake, and serenades the spawning brook trout.

Sometimes the way in is not the best way out. Instead of the steep slope that carried us quickly to the lake's shore, we take a lower route that feeds us out into a series of ravines and stream crossings some of which we will take by walking atop fallen trees. I am midway across one of these natural bridges when I turn to Caleb, who is crossing the same stream by another fallen tree, and ask if Carhartt is following me. She is. I feel young at knowing this. I feel young at walking lengths of trees, even though there is no other way. There is a joy in this. A deep joy in doing it with those I call family. I store this moment in a place where I also hold the wistfulness for the season, and the meadow, the spring. I store it with the knowing that one day I will look back with yearning and with the knowledge that Caleb and I, and Carhartt and Cisco, and this place will never be again as we are now. Never as young. Never as new to this place. Never again to see it for the first time. The four of us regroup and follow each other single file, into the downed trees. The dogs are seemingly more subdued as if they, too, sense the summer's end.

The more downed trees I must cross the more I smile. In my forty-sixth year, I have never felt surer in my body. I have hiked countless miles this summer. Slept countless nights beside streams and rivers, at trailheads, at lakes without names. From this year forward I will carry a scar on my knee from the granite above French Creek Lake where daydreaming became a lesson in humility, an exchange I made with skin and blood. When I am feeling the miles in my bones, I will remind myself of the seventy-nine-year-old woman I met this summer who, after having her femurs broken in a winter accident a couple of years earlier, had just hiked forty-odd miles in two days. As she was walking away, I turned to Caleb and told him that is all I want from this life, to be able to keep walking in these mountains.

We reach the truck just as the wind picks up. I have all day waited to hear a tree fall on the slope around us. A burn here in 1997 left steeples of sub-alpine fir whose roots are certainly rotten by now. But they, like their cousin the whitebark pine, are not quick to give up their post. One last look toward where I cannot see the meadow, then back at the landscape we just walked, I get in the truck, and we drive the road that takes us home.

Indian Summer. I keep hearing it in my mind. Maybe it is becoming a mantra. An incantation. Perhaps I am trying to call such an autumn forth. A chance to be wrong about this last hike. To find a late September weekend when, finally, we do make our way back to the meadow. To the place where I lay my cheek in the silver of the Hard Butte stream and drink. Where I watch Carhartt chase what she imagines as her foe, jumping easily from log to log, Cisco on her tail. Caleb beside me. Maybe Indian Summer is a sign that I am tracing with my lips, a sign like the one at Summit Lake, like the smell of elk musk, like the crimson of the brook trout. Another chance at discovery. For awe. To make good on that wish to grow old hiking these Salmon River ridges. To finally explain a feeling that words cannot seem to define.

This Bend in the River or What May Have Been a Dream

You might come here on a Tuesday. To the trail, to this bench, to this place where the willows and sand and gravel meet the edge of history. Your history and the rivers. At this bend.

It's the end of something. Or the beginning. And you need a place that is reserved. Reserved, not in the sense of "just for you" but reserved as in "holding back a little." Somewhere aside. Off to the side. A place to watch from. So you can see, as you do now, the child in her red jacket. The lilac skirt as it flutters against the woman's knees. Birds whose names you promised to learn but have yet to find the time to do so, and it aches you to know that you have put this simple task so far down now, so far down on the to-do list.

And there goes the dog chasing the stick the water has worn smooth. For a moment you bound along with her, your own fur bouncing, and think that maybe it's finally time for another dog. A new dog. You remember that joy of watching wagging. Of the welcome home. Yes, maybe it is time. You lean back against the bench thinking about time, and the dog runs from view and is soon forgotten or forsaken like the water bowl you placed on the shelf in the closet.

You are far enough from the river to see it as an owl might, as the past might, but from the height of a willow. It is dawn, or it is early evening. The summer heat is pressing, more pressing than you remember from other, younger days on the river. Other bends. Before the dams. You wonder if, sitting here, you breathe in the exhalations of fish. You ask, are there salmon in this river? The alders answer. The cottonwood answer and their answer is enough. Isn't this why you have come here? For enough? To be in a place that is with and without. Here the climbing and struggling is merely an ant upon your trouser leg with nothing to sell. No agenda. A being that sees you as a thing to be wandered, explored. Tastes that drop of honey, or was it hummingbird nectar, that dripped off your finger at a time when a sweet need of another was what you filled.

You draw a circle with your toe and watch the earth fall in. You wish your scuffing would uncover an arrowhead. You know it is cliché, but you long to find one. Not because your pockets are empty, but because to hold an arrowhead would help you remember that others have come here and have left their wisdom, and, like them, you want to leave something of value. Something useful. To not be forgotten. Something that someone might uncover with an *oh* and remember what it feels like to be filled with wonder and mystery and curiosity, something that brings them to their knees in search of more. You think you may have something in common with the person who left that arrowhead. Maybe it is a love of rivers. Maybe they, too, liked the smell of wet rocks and cottonwood resin.

You wish to throw a rock and hear the splash. You remember what it meant to be a child at the river. To bring your bare soles to the seam. But even then, you understood choices. Other's fear. The danger of going too far in the swift stream. But you could not help it. We all want to get carried away. Sometimes. Where are those skipped rocks now? Those chances and splashes? Where is the fishing pole and your mother's sack lunches and that lover who loved to make love beside water? A couple flutters a quilt to the sand and lies down. In your mind, you lie down, too.

When you were small, you thought that rivers were meant to take things away. The stick you threw, the ball, that plaything you let go of. You saw floods. The house carried away. The logs, the road. You saw fish float from baited hooks. Even snow and ice were carried down, down. If the river can take, can it also bring back? You know the river brought you here. To this bend.

And now the clouds must be gathering. Or perhaps the sun has dropped below the horizon, or you are just growing older, tired, but it is darker. You rise and walk finally to the river's edge. You see sky reflected there. The blue of it. The light left shimmering in water. The children have gone home for their suppers. The lovers moved back into the trees. In the distance, a dog barks, and the dog and the lovers and the child in the red jacket and even the woman in the lilac skirt are never there at all. This is why you have come to the river. You and these memories. You and every river you have ever known. Ever loved. Weren't they all the life you wanted to be part of? Weren't each of the rivers what you craved from life? To bring life? To bring and be carried away? To be useful and beautiful and to have shores that would gather others?

And here it still is. And it is not too late. Not too late to take off your shoes. Your coat will be on the bench where you leave it. We will all be here with you, all of us, arrowheads pressed in our palms, dogs at our sides, wading together, into the gush of cool, feeling the smooth of stones skipped for centuries, the salmon returning past breeched dams bringing us together like pebbles into a redd. A community, a family, kin holding on to one another, gathering at this bend and with all the river brings.

Acknowledgments

This book is the product of a collective effort and much of my graduate thesis from the University of Idaho MFA program. I am thankful to the editors and readers of these publications in which previous versions of the following essays have appeared: "Along the Salmon River," *Backcountry Journal*; "Coyote Story," *Emergence Magazine* and *Evergreen: Grim Tales & Verses from the Gloomy Northwest*; "Aspen," *High Desert Journal*; "Hells Canyon Revival," *Sustainable Play, GetLit Anthology, & Freeflow*; "Lake 8," *Platform Review*; "Letter Born of a Snowy Morning," *Torrey House Water Anthology*; "No Way to Say Goodbye," winner of the Walter Nathan Essay award from the University of Minnesota.

Thank you to Bloedel Reserve for awarding me with a residency and time to consider what this collection may look like as a book. Thank you to the Idaho Commission on the Arts for awarding me a two-year tenure as an Idaho Writer in Residence, which offered resources and travel throughout the state of Idaho.

Thank you to Jeffrey Levine of Tupelo Press for seeing the potential in bib overalls and timidity in Truchas, New Mexico.

Thanks to Laura Pritchett for inspiring "Letter Born of a Snowy Morning" and being such a careful and thoughtful reader of my work as well as a champion for my voice (and sometimes silences.)

Thank you to Linda Hogan for calling to make sure I was writing and believing me and believing in me.

Thank you to Doug Peacock who read "Hells Canyon Revival" and handed it back to me with only the words "publish this" written on the top—and for taking me out to the desert both literally and figuratively—and showing me that the lives are always there. And for always reminding me that the experience is more important than the story. And to Andrea Peacock, who keeps us all upright and moving forward. And thank you to Bill Kittredge who read and commented on the same essay and said, "It's not what you think it is about," then left it at the bar.

Thank you to Jennifer S. Anderson who asked me to be the Stegner Lecturer at Lewis and Clark State College, which inspired me to write about road decommissioning and hope.

Thank you to Colorado Public Radio, particularly Erin Robertson, Rebeka Romberg, Brad Turner, and Kibwe Cooper for the wonderful idea of the *Terra Firma* Podcast where snippets of some of these stories live alongside the sound recordings of Jacob Job. I am so honored.

To Allen Gee, my trusted friend and insightful editor: your keen eye and thoughtful suggestions have shaped these stories into their truest form. I am deeply grateful for your unwavering support and friendship.

To Harry W. Greene, my herpetological mentor: your gentle guidance and vast knowledge have transformed my fear into fascination.

To Stacy Boe Miller, my soul's poet laureate and always my first reader, whose advice and corrections I take without question.

Thank you to my teachers, mentors, and friends, whom I could (and maybe should) write an entire book about. To mention a few: Kim Barnes, Robert Wrigley, Alexandra Teague, Mike McGriff, Brian Blanchfield, Tyson Hausdoerffer, Debra Gwartney, Kim Stafford, Sarah Goettsch, Jennifer Baillargeon (I love you), Gary Dorr, Ciarra Greene, Julian Ankney, my UI cohort and Sam Burns, Cass Cleghorn, Tammy Ota, Sharma Shields, Maya Jewell Zeller, my friends at *The Inlander*, Carhartt (always Carhartt), Janet Hohmann, the Payette National Forest, J. Drew Lanham, Elizabeth Bradfield, Derek Sheffield, and every single student who I've shared a wild, virtual, or brick and mortar classroom with. Thank you.

Nathan, thank you. I love you.

Mostly, thank you to this land which I have learned from. This land and its beings who have shown me the way to my stories, who have taught me about voice, who have proven that sometimes the way in, is by going out.

First and foremost, to Caleb, my unwavering companion on this Idaho adventure: thank you for your love, patience, and unwavering belief in my dreams. I love this life we have made together.

And always and forever my deepest gratitude to my dad, Ronald Fuhrman, who was a man made of story and always offered me more; my sister, Janet Fuhrman, who will tell you she is thoroughly responsible for all the writing that I have ever done ☺; and to my mom, Dolores Fuhrman, who has made every good thing that has happened in my life possible through her love, unfaltering generosity, and willingness to adopt me.

About the author

CMarie Fuhrman is the author of *Camped Beneath the Dam: Poems* and co-editor of the PNBA, IPPY and IP award winning anthology *Cascadia: Art, Ecology, Poetry* and also co-editor of *Native Voices: Indigenous Poetry, Craft, and Conversations*. She is the winner of the Walter Nathan Essay Award and is an award-winning columnist for the *Inlander* and Director of the Elk River Writers Workshop. She is Associate Director and Director of Poetry at Western Colorado University, where she teaches nature writing. CMarie is also the host of the podcast *Terra Firma*. She is a former Idaho Writer in Residence and lives in the Salmon River Mountains of Idaho.

The Donald L. Jordan Endowment was established in 2016, in part, to facilitate the formation of Columbus State University Press, which was officially formed in 2021. CSU Press is pleased to recognize Mr. Jordan as the founder of the press, which serves as the publishing venue for the Donald L. Jordan Prize for Literary Excellence, and for The Nature Series at DLJ Books. DLJ Books has been installed as a permanent imprint at the press. Mr. Jordan's foresight made CSU Press a reality, and we are grateful for his generosity. Mr. Jordan passed away on May 15, 2023 after a very successful business career. The author of literary novels, short stories, and works of non-fiction, he was also particularly interested in helping other writers attain publication.

www.ingramcontent.com/pod-product-compliance
Lightning Source LLC
Chambersburg PA
CBHW031958010726
47493CB00007B/2252